The Plutarch Project
Volume Three

The Plutarch Project
Volume Three

Julius Caesar, Agis and Cleomenes, and the Gracchi

by

Anne E. White

ISBN-13 978-0-9947977-8-0

CONTENTS

Introduction

These notes, and the accompanying text, are prepared specifically for the use of AmblesideOnline students following a twelve-week term, who need passages of a readable length along with a bit of vocabulary and background help. The text is that of Thomas North's 1579 translation of Plutarch's *Lives of the Noble Greeks and Romans*, with some substitutions from John Dryden's 1683 translation [in brackets]. I have updated spelling, and occasionally punctuation. There are also a number of omissions, either for length or for suitability, which are *not* always noted. I do not intend this to irritate purists and academics, but simply to provide an edited version of the story that will be useful for individual students and small groups, while remaining as respectful as possible to the original text. Likewise, the historic dates are incomplete, and are included only to give an idea of important events and the passage of time.

Using the Study Guide

Some lessons are divided into two or three sections. These can be read all at once, or used throughout the week. The vocabulary lists are there to save time on having to look things up, or to explain puzzles like the word "let," which can mean either "allow" or "prevent." The word "curious" is another puzzle to modern ears. It appears three times in North's translation of *The Gracchi*, used in a slightly different context each time, and none of those have the meanings that we give to the word (e.g. to be curious or inquisitive about something, or to find something curious or strange). The one similar usage in more recent language is when we read that something was of "curious design," which we might assume to mean strange or peculiar, but which actually means finely detailed.

A Special Note on the Introductory Material

Each study contains some explanatory material before the first lesson begins. The parent/teacher should look through this before beginning the study, and choose when or how to present the material. A little at the beginning of the first lesson may be useful to stir interest in the new study, but it is not meant to be given all in one dose! Some of the information may be more helpful as you introduce later lessons, or to answer questions that the students ask.

I encourage you to make the lessons your own. Use the discussion questions that are the most meaningful to you. But remember that Charlotte Mason was satisfied with "Proper names are written on the blackboard, and then the children narrate what they have listened to."

Finally...

You may notice that some of the questions come from a specifically Christian worldview. I do not apologize for that, but I do think it's fair to mention it. Those with other beliefs may find similar references within their own faith traditions.

A note of thanks

Thank you to the group of AmblesideOnline users who field-tested these notes. Special thanks to those attending the 2016 L'Harmas Charlotte Mason Gathering in Kingsville, Ontario, who contributed vocabulary suggestions and discussion questions for Lesson Seven of *The Gracchi*.

Julius Caesar
(July 13, 100 B.C.—March 15, 44 B.C.)

Who Was Gaius Julius Caesar?

Julius Caesar was a political leader and general during the last days of the Roman Republic. Over his long career, he held every possible high civic, military, and even religious position in Rome. He was also a noted **orator** and writer. (An **orator** was a public speaker, usually someone who used those skills in political or legal matters.)

Who were Sulla and Marius?

When Julius Caesar was about sixteen, a civil war began between two mighty Roman rivals: **Lucias Cornelius Sulla**, and Caesar's uncle-by-marriage, **Gaius Marius**, who was allied with another leader named **Lucius Cornelius Cinna.** Several personal events happened in Caesar's life at the same time: his father died, leaving him as head of the family; he nominated himself to be the High Priest of Jupiter (see the note below); and he was married to Cinna's daughter Cornelia. When Sulla's side gained power in Rome, Caesar (as a "Marian," or sympathizer with Marius) not only lost his position and inheritance, and was pressured to divorce his wife, but had to go into hiding as well. Even when the threat to his life ended, Caesar thought he would be safer away from Rome, so he joined military expeditions in Asia and Cilicia. It has been noted that that Rome was the real

1

beneficiary of Caesar's "career change," since, as the High Priest of Jupiter (a special position that had many restrictions attached to it), he would not have been allowed to participate in the military.

A note on the spelling of Sulla: North and Dryden spell this name "Sylla," although other sources spell it "Sulla." The reason is that Plutarch wrote in Greek, and "Sylla" was his Greek version of the Latin name. I have used "Sulla" to avoid confusion.

Who were Caesar's wives?

As noted above, Caesar's first wife was Cornelia the daughter of Cinna; his second was Pompeia, the granddaughter of Sulla; and his third was Calpurnia, the one featured in Shakespeare's play. He was also engaged to another girl before his first marriage, but the rules of the priesthood required him to marry someone whose family was of equal rank to his.

What was the priesthood of Jupiter? What was *Pontifex Maximus*?

Thomas North often used images from his own culture to translate Greek and Roman terms. Knights defended castles (forts); men opened their doublets (see **Lesson Eleven**) and rode in carriages (chariots); and the high priest became a bishop. For our purposes, it is necessary only to know that there were numerous levels and types of priesthood in Rome and throughout the rest of Italy; and that these positions carried political as well as spiritual authority. Julius Caesar became a *pontifex* (priest) in 73 B.C., after the death of Sulla; and *Pontifex Maximus* (chief or high priest) in 63 B.C. These were different positions from his original title of High Priest of Jupiter, and did not keep him from military leadership.

(The Latin word *pontifex* crossed over to English in words such as "pontiff" and "to pontificate.")

What was an aedile, a quaestor, a consul?

The elected positions or magistracies in Rome were (starting at the bottom): quaestor, aedile, praetor, and consul. (The office of tribune was a separate position, explained in the *Lives of the Gracchi*.) Ex-consuls could become censors, and a consul could become dictator if the need (usually a great emergency) arose.

Who were the Gauls and the Germans?

One of Julius Caesar's major contributions to the Roman Republic (soon to be the Roman Empire) was to enlarge its boundaries by taking over new territory in Europe. Throughout the story, we have the names (usually in North's spelling) of numerous tribes and sub-tribes, some of them Gauls, others Germans, but all of them seen as potential Roman soldiers/taxpayers. For reasons of space, the names of these tribes are not included in the vocabulary.

Who was Pompey?

Gnaeus Pompeius Magnus, or **Pompey the Great**, was a military and political leader, famous for his exploits in Sulla's Second Civil War. His marriage to Caesar's daughter Julia might have eased the rivalry between them, but her early death ended that possibility.

Who were all those other people whose names started with "C?"

Casca: Two Casca brothers were involved in the assassination of Caesar: **Publius Servilius Casca Longus**, who struck the first blow; and **Gaius Servilius Casca**, a close friend of Caesar's.

Marcus Licinius Crassus, called Crassus: a Roman general and politician (115 B.C.-53 B.C.), one of the First Triumvirate with Caesar and Pompey; he was also known for his wealth.

Cassius: Gaius Cassius Longinus, a brother-in-law of Brutus, was a Roman senator and one of the conspirators against Caesar.

Cato: Marcus Porcius Cato Uticensis, or Cato the Younger, was a statesman who had frequent conflicts of opinion with Caesar. His son, **Marcus Porcius Cato**, was a brother-in-law to Brutus, and died at the Battle of Philippi in 42 B.C.

Cicero: Quintus Tullius Cicero was a military leader during Caesar's Gallic wars. **Marcus Tullius Cicero**, his older brother, was a Roman statesman and **orator** (see introductory note), and was put to death in 43 B.C. because of his enmity to **Marcus Antonius**. (Because Shakespeare called **Marcus Antonius** by the anglicized **Mark or Marc Antony**, we often use that name. Plutarch refers to him simply as **Antonius**.)

Cinna: there are several Cinnas in the story, beginning with **Lucius Cornelius Cinna (the Elder)**, Caesar's first father-in-law. Then we have **Lucius Cornelius Cinna (the Younger)**, one of the conspirators against Caesar; and **Helvius Cinna** or "Cinna the Poet," whose name led to an unfortunate misunderstanding.

Should we read Shakespeare's Julius Caesar at the same time?

In the original PNEU schools, students read William Shakespeare's play *The Tragedy of Julius Caesar* in the same term as Plutarch's *Life of Julius Caesar*. And why not? One lends interest to the other, and seeing what an expert dramatist created with his source material is a wonderful lesson in writing. The problem is that the play focuses on the last days of Caesar's life, the conspiracy and assassination; with a shift at the end to Cassius and Brutus. If students are familar with the story, they may not find it too confusing to jump so far ahead of their Plutarch readings. An alternative, not traditional for Charlotte Mason, but workable especially for younger students, might be to focus on Plutarch for the first part of the term; and then read the play.

Notes on the play (Shakespeare Connections) are included in the last few lessons of this study.

Lesson One

Introduction

In a time when many in Rome were being put to death for their political loyalties (or even for being related to the wrong party), young Julius Caesar was on the wrong side. Most people, realizing that, would have stayed hidden or at least tried to live quietly; but Julius Caesar was never most people. In fact, he decided to put himself forward for the very public position of High Priest of Jupiter. Sulla, who had recently won a civil war and become dictator of Rome, had been too busy to worry much about one teenage boy with Marian connections; but that got his immediate attention, and now Caesar was in trouble.

Vocabulary

the country of the Sabines: a mountainous area northeast of Rome

being carried from house to house, in a **litter:** on a bed or couch which was carried on poles by servants

talent: a unit of money

Isle of Pharmacusa: a small Greek island in the Aegean Sea

Cilicia: an ancient kingdom that is now part of Turkey

had the spoil of their goods: looted their possessions

praetor: the office of praetor could include governorship of a province

more ceremonious: Dryden, "tact and consideration beyond what could have been expected at his age"

he ever kept a good board: he was hospitable

liberal: generous

quail: falter, weaken

underfoot: Dryden says "broken and in a low condition"

the state of the commonwealth: the way things were governed

People

Sulla: Sulla was made Perpetual Dictator, but resigned after one year, and was elected as consul instead for 80 B.C., along with Metellus Pius, whom Caesar later replaced as *Pontifex Maximus*.

Marcus Juncus: North's translation has it "Iunius," and Dryden "Junius," but modern sources say that Caesar dealt with Marcus Juncus, the governor of Asia in 75 B.C.

Historic Occasions

75 B.C.: Caesar's kidnapping by pirates

67 B.C.: Caesar returned from Spain and married Pompeia

Reading

Part One

When [Sulla] was determined to have killed [Caesar], some of his friends told him, that it was to no purpose to put so young a boy as he to death. But Sulla told them again, that they did not consider that there were many Marians in that young boy. Caesar understanding that, stole out of Rome, and hid himself a long time in **the country of the Sabines**, wandering still from place to place. But one day **being carried from house to house**, he fell into the hands of Sulla's soldiers, who searched all those places, and took them whom they found hidden. Caesar bribed the captain, whose name was Cornelius, with two **talents** which he gave him.

After he had escaped them thus, he went unto the seaside, and took ship, and sailed into Bithynia to go unto King Nicomedes. When he had been with him awhile, he took [to] sea again, and was taken by pirates about the **Isle of Pharmacusa**: for those pirates kept all upon that seacoast, with a great fleet of ships and boats. They asking him at the first twenty **talents** for his ransom, Caesar laughed them to scorn, as though they knew not what a man they had taken, and of himself promised them fifty **talents**. Then he sent his men up and down to get him this money, so that he was left in manner alone among these thieves of the **Cilicians**, (which are the cruellest butchers in the world) with one of his friends, and two of his slaves only: and yet he made so little reckoning of them, that when he was desirous to sleep, he sent unto them to command them to make no noise.

Thus was he eight and thirty days among them, not kept as

prisoner, but rather waited upon by them as a prince. All this time he would boldly exercise himself in any sport or pastime they would go to. And otherwhile also he would write verses, and make orations, and call them together to say them before them: and if any of them seemed as though they had not understood him, or passed not for them, he called them blockheads, and brute beasts, and laughing, threatened them that he would hang them up. But they were as merry with the matter as could be, and took all in good part, thinking that this his bold speech came through the simplicity of his youth.

So when his ransom was come from the city of Miletum, they being paid their money, and he again set at liberty he then presently armed, and manned out certain ships out of the haven of Miletum, to follow those thieves, whom he found yet riding at anchor in the same island. So he took the most of them, and **had the spoil of their goods**, but for their bodies, he brought them into the city of Pergamum, and there committed them to prison, whilst he himself went to speak with **Marcus Juncus**, who had the government of Asia, as unto whom the execution of these pirates did belong, for that he was **praetor** of that country. But this **praetor** having a great fancy to be fingering of the money, because there was good store of it, answered that he would consider of these prisoners at better leisure. Caesar leaving **Juncus** there, returned again unto Pergamum, and there hung up all these thieves openly upon a cross, as he had oftentimes promised them in the isle he would do, when they thought he did but jest.

Part Two

[Caesar spent some time studying in Rhodes, and then returned to Rome. He became active in public life, taking cases as a lawyer.]

Now Caesar immediately won many men's good wills at Rome, through his eloquence in pleading of their causes: and the people loved him marvellously also, because of the courteous manner he had to speak to every man, and to use them gently, being **more ceremonious** therein than was looked for in one of his years.

Furthermore, **he ever kept a good board**, and fared well at his table, and was very **liberal** besides: the which indeed did advance him forward, and brought him in estimation with the people. His enemies judg[ed] that this favour of the common people would soon **quail**, when he could no longer hold out that charge and expense, [so they] suffered him to run on, till by little and little he was grown to be of great strength and power. But in fine, when they had thus given him the bridle to grow to this greatness, and that they could not then pull him back, though indeed in sight it would turn one day to the destruction of the whole state and commonwealth of Rome: too late they found, that there is not so little a beginning of anything, but continuance of time will soon make it strong, when through contempt there is no impediment to hinder the greatness.

Part Three

[Caesar became first a tribune [72 B.C.] and then treasurer, or quaestor [68/67 B.C.], and aedile [65 B.C.]. He lost his wife Cornelia, but then married again.]

At that time there were two factions in Rome, to wit, the faction of Sulla, which was very strong and of great power, and the other of Marius, which then was **underfoot** and durst not shew itself. [And to this end, whilst he was in the height of his repute with the people for the magnificent shows he gave as aedile, he ordered images of Marius and figures of Victory, with trophies in their hands, to be carried privately in the night and placed in the Capitol.] The next morning when every man saw the glistering of these golden images excellently well wrought, shewing by the inscriptions that they were the victories which Marius had won upon the Cimbres: everyone marvelled much at the boldness of him that durst set them up there, knowing well enough who it was. Hereupon, it ran straight through all the city, and every man came thither to see them. Then some cried out upon Caesar, and said it was a tyranny which he meant to set up, by renewing of such honours as before had been trodden under foot, and forgotten, by common decree and open proclamation: and that it was no more but a bait to gauge the people's good wills, which he had set out in the stately shews of his common plays, to see if he had brought them to his lure, that they would abide such parts to be played, and a new alteration of things to be made.

They of Marius' faction on the other side, encouraging one another, shewed themselves straight a great number gathered together, and made the Mount of the Capitol ring again with their cries and clapping of hands: insomuch as the tears ran down many of their cheeks for very joy, when they saw the images of Marius, and they extolled Caesar to the skies, judging him the worthiest man of all the kindred of Marius.

The Senate being assembled thereupon, Catulus Luctatius, one of the greatest authority at that time in Rome, rose, and vehemently inveighed against Caesar, and spake that then which ever since hath been noted much: that Caesar did not now covertly go to work, but by plain force sought to alter **the state of the commonwealth**. [Dryden: *that Caesar was now not working mines, but planting batteries to overthrow the state.*] Nevertheless, Caesar at that time answered him so that the Senate was satisfied. Thereupon they that had him in estimation did grow in better hope than before, and persuaded him, that hardily he should give place to no man, and that through the goodwill of the people, he should be better than all [of them], and come to be the chiefest man of the city.

Narration and Discussion

The pirate story ends in quite a gruesome way. What impression do you get here of Julius Caesar?

Dryden translates the last sentence in **Part Two** this way: "When his power at last was established and not to be overthrown, and now openly tended to the altering of the whole constitution, they were aware too late that there is no beginning so mean [*little*], which continued application will not make considerable, and that despising a danger at first will make it at last irresistible." What is the danger in ignoring a small problem? Can you think of any Scriptures that support this? (Song of Solomon 2:15)

Lesson Two

Introduction

From quaestor and aedile to *Pontifex Maximus*, praetor, and finally consul: was there any higher that Caesar could go?

Vocabulary

chief bishop: *Pontifex Maximus* (see introductory notes)

room: position

made suit for it, sued for something: ran for the position

importunate: pressing, impatient

boldness and courage: Dryden: "youthful vigour and heat"

commonwealth: a group or union of states or countries that work together, in this case Rome and its provinces and colonies

surety: one taking financial responsibility

suffered: allowed

footmen: foot soldiers

the great sea Oceanum: *Mare Oceanum*, the Atlantic Ocean

triumph: an official parade in celebration of a military victory

let the triumph fall: let it pass, drop it

device: strategy

at jar: in conflict

gainsaying: interfering, preventing

People

Isauricus: father of the **Isauricus** who was co-consul with Caesar

Pompey and Crassus: Pompey, Crassus, and Caesar together are called the First Triumvirate or "rule of three men."

Cato: see introductory notes

Historic Occasions

63 B.C.: Caesar became *Pontifex Maximus*

62 B.C.: Caesar served as praetor and governor of Spain

60 B.C.: Caesar was elected consul along with Marcus Bibulus

Reading

Part One

At that time, the **chief bishop** Metellus died, and two of the notablest men of the city, and of greatest authority (**Isauricus** and Catulus) contended for his **room**: Caesar notwithstanding their contention, would give neither of them place, but presented himself to the people, and **made suit for it** as they did. The suit being equal betwixt either of them, Catulus, because he was a man of greater calling and dignity than the other, doubting the uncertainty of the election: sent unto Caesar a good sum of money, to make him leave off his suit. But Caesar sent him word again, that he would [borrow] a greater sum than that, to maintain the suit against him.

When the day of the election came, his mother bringing him to the door of his house, Caesar weeping, kissed her, and said, "Mother, this day thou shalt see thy son **chief bishop** of Rome, or banished from Rome." In fine, when the voices of the people were gathered together, and the strife well debated: Caesar won the victory, and made the Senate and noble men all afraid of him, for that they thought that thenceforth he would make the people do what he thought good.

Part Two

[Caesar made some powerful enemies during the Catiline Conspiracy crisis, when he argued against putting criminals of noble families to death. But shortly afterwards, he became praetor.]

The government of the province of Spain being fallen unto Caesar for that he was praetor: his creditors came and cried out upon him, and were **importunate** of him to be paid. Caesar being unable to satisfy them, was compelled to go unto **Crassus**, who was the richest man of all Rome, and that stood in need of Caesar's **boldness and courage** to withstand **Pompey's** greatness in the **commonwealth**.

Crassus became his **surety** unto his greediest creditors for the sum of eight hundred and thirty talents: whereupon they **suffered** Caesar to depart to the government of his province.

In his journey it is reported that, passing over the mountains of the Alps, they came through a little poor village that had not many households, and yet poor cottages. There, his friends that did accompany him, asked him merrily, if there were any contending for offices in that town, and whether there were any strife there amongst the noble men for honour. Caesar speaking in good earnest, answered: "I cannot tell that," said he, "but for my part, I had rather be the chiefest man here, than the second person in Rome."

Another time also when he was in Spain, reading the history of Alexander's acts, when he had read it, he was sorrowful a good while after, and then burst out in weeping. His friends, seeing that, marvelled what should be the cause of his sorrow. "Do ye not think," said he, "that I have good cause to be heavy, when King Alexander being no older than myself is now, had in old time won so many nations and countries: and that I hitherunto have done nothing worthy of myself?"

Therefore when he was come into Spain, he was very careful of his business, and had in few days joined ten new ensigns more of **footmen** unto the other twenty which he had before. Then marching forward against the Callaecians and Lusitanians, he conquered all, and went as far as **the great sea Oceanum**, subduing all the people which before knew not the Romans for their lords. There he took order for pacifying of the war, and did as wisely take order for the establishing of peace. For he did reconcile the cities together, and made them friends one with another, but specially he pacified all suits of law, and strife, betwixt the debtors and creditors, which [had grown] by reason of usury. For he ordained that the creditors should take yearly two parts of the revenue of their debtors, until such time as they had paid themselves: and that the debtors should have the third part to themselves to live withal. He having won great estimation by this good order taken, returned from his government very rich, and his soldiers also [were] full of rich spoils, who called him Imperator, [that is] to say, sovereign captain.

Part Three

*[Caesar now had a problem. He was in line for a military **triumph**, but he also wanted to run for consul, and the rules for the two contradicted each other.]*

Now the Romans having a custom, that such as demanded honour of **triumph**, should remain awhile without the city, and that they on the other side which sued for the consulship, should of necessity be there in person: Caesar coming unhappily at that very time when the consuls were chosen, he sent to pray the Senate to do him that favour, that being absent, he might by his friends sue for the consulship. **Cato** at the first did vehemently inveigh against it, vouching an express law forbidding the contrary. But afterwards, perceiving that notwithstanding the reasons he alleged, many of the senators (being won by Caesar) favoured his request: yet he cunningly sought all he could to prevent [and delay] them.

Caesar thereupon determined rather to [**let the triumph fall**], and to make suit for the consulship: and so came into the city, and had such a **device** with him, as went beyond them all [except for] **Cato**. His **device** was this: **Pompey and Crassus**, two of the greatest personages of the city of Rome, being **at jar** together, Caesar made them friends, and by that means got unto himself the power of them both: for, by colour of that gentle act and friendship of his, he subtly (unawares to them all) did greatly alter and [caused what was in effect a revolution in the government].

Thus Caesar being brought unto the assembly of the election, in the midst of these two noble persons, whom he had before reconciled together: he was there chosen consul, with Calpurnius Bibulus, without **gainsaying** or contradiction of any man.

Narration and Discussion

Caesar speaking in good earnest, answered: "I cannot tell that," said he, "but for my part, I had rather be the chiefest man here, than the second person in Rome." What did he mean?

Discuss Caesar's reaction to his reading of Alexander. Should the stories of heroes make us weep?

Why was Caesar's reconciliation of Pompey and Crassus actually a play for power? Can peacemaking ever be a bad thing?

Creative Narration: Interview the newly-elected consul Julius Caesar. You may wish to review his past history, ask him about his plans as consul, and perhaps something about how he is going to deal with his political opponents.

Lesson Three

Introduction

The year 59 B.C. was referred to afterwards as the "Consulship of Julius and Caesar." In this political soap opera, alliances between the heavyweights alternated with smear campaigns and backstabbing. Votes, or "voices," could be easily bought—or lost. By the end of the year, Caesar was badly in need of something that would regain the Romans' trust and respect. (A war might work.)

What ailed Caesar?

Because of Plutarch's comments, there is a belief that Julius Caesar had "the falling sickness," or epilepsy. However, medical scholars have not agreed on what sort of seizures or spells of weakness he had, or what caused them.

Vocabulary

he was entered into his office: he was acting officially as consul

meeter for a seditious tribune of the people: that would better have been proposed by an audacious tribune

preferred the division of lands: proposed a redistribution of land (outside the city) that would give property to veteran soldiers

gratis: free

device: the strategy he proposed

having Crassus on the one side...: this was a public declaration that the three had teamed up together

to let him: to prevent him

target: shield

unmeet for his gravity, uncomely: undignified, disrespectful

which was made sure before; was sure: was engaged to be married

empire of Rome: there was no official Roman Empire yet, since there was no emperor, so this is a general term

the marketplace: the Roman Forum

legion: a Roman military unit then made up of about 4500 men

attended the house: came to meetings of the Senate

prowess: skill

subject to headache, and otherwhile to the falling sickness: see note on this (above)

soberly: plainly, without luxury

by writing ciphers in letters: the Roman writer Suetonius wrote this about Caesar: "... if he had anything confidential to say, he wrote it in cipher, that is, by so changing the order of the letters of the alphabet, that not a word could be made out." This type of substitution cipher is still called a Caesar Cipher.

sparage: asparagus

People

Piso: Lucius Calpurnius Piso Caesoninus (c. 100 BC – 43 BC), consul in 58 B.C. He is known for his antagonism to **Marcus Tullius Cicero**.

Calpurnius Bibulus: the son-in-law of **Cato**

P. Claudius: Claudius had "party-crashed" a women's ceremony at Julius Caesar's house, which was a serious matter and caused Caesar to divorce his wife. Like **Piso**, Claudius was an enemy of **Cicero**.

Reading

Part One

Now when **he was entered into his office**, he began to put forth laws **meeter for a seditious tribune of the people**, than for a consul: because by them he **preferred the division of lands**, and distributing of corn to every citizen **gratis**, to please [the common people]. But when the noble men of the Senate were against his **device**, he desiring no better occasion, began to cry out, and to protest, that by the overhardness and austerity of the Senate, they drove him against his will to lean unto the people: and thereupon **having Crassus on the one side of him, and Pompey on the other**, he asked [the two of] them openly in the assembly, if they did give their consent unto the laws which he had put forth. They both answered, they did. Then he prayed them to stand by him against those that threatened him with force of sword **to let him**. Crassus gave him his word, he would. Pompey also did the like, and added thereunto, that he would come with his sword and **target** both, against them that would withstand him with their swords. These words offended much the Senate, being far **unmeet for his gravity**, and indecent for the majesty and honour he carried, and most of all **uncomely** for the presence of the Senate whom he should have reverenced: and were speeches fitter for a rash light-headed youth, than for his person. Howbeit the common people on the other side, they rejoiced.

Then Caesar, because he would be more assured of Pompey's power and friendship, he gave him his daughter Julia in marriage, **which was made sure before** unto Servilius Caepio, and promised him [Servilius] in exchange, Pompey's [daughter], the which **was sure** also unto Faustus the son of Sulla. And shortly after also, Caesar [him]self did marry Calpurnia the daughter of **Piso**, whom he caused to be made consul, to succeed him the next year following. **Cato** then cried out with open mouth, and called the gods to witness, that it was a shameful matter, and not to be suffered, that they should in that sort make havoc of the **empire of Rome**, distributing among themselves, through those wicked marriages, the governments of the provinces, and of great armies. **Calpurnius Bibulus**, fellow consul with Caesar, perceiving that he did contend in vain, making all the resistance he could to withstand this law, and that oftentimes he was in danger to be slain with **Cato**, in **the marketplace** and assembly: he kept close in his house all the rest of his consulship.

When Pompey had married Julia, he filled all the marketplace with soldiers, and by open force authorized the laws which Caesar made in the behalf of the people. Furthermore, [he secured Caesar the government of all Gaul], and beyond the Alps, and all Illyria, with four **legions** granted him for five years. Then Cato standing up to speak against it: Caesar bade his officers lay hold of him, and carry him to prison, thinking he would have appealed unto the tribunes. But Cato said never a word, when he went his way. Caesar perceiving then, that not only the senators and nobility were offended, but that the common people also for the reverence they bare unto Cato's virtues, were ashamed, and went away with silence: he himself secretly did pray one of the tribunes that he would take Cato from the officers. [As for the other senators, some few of them **attended the house**, the rest, being disgusted, absented themselves.]

The shamefullest part that Caesar played while he was consul, seemeth to be this: when he chose **P. Claudius** tribune of the people, (that had offered his wife such dishonour, and profaned the holy ancient mysteries of the women, which were celebrated in his own house). **Claudius** sued to be tribune to no other end but to destroy **Cicero**: and Caesar [him]self also departed not from Rome to his army, before he had set them together by the ears, and driven Cicero out of Italy.

Part Two

All these things they say he did, before the wars with the Gauls. But the time of the great armies and conquests he made afterwards, and of the war in the which he subdued all the Gauls: (entering into another course of life far contrary unto the first) made him to be known for as valiant a soldier and as excellent a captain to lead men, as those that afore him had been counted the wisest and most valiantest generals that ever were, and that by their valiant deeds had achieved great honour. For whosoever would compare the house of the Fabians, of the Scipioes, of the Metellians, yea those also of his own time, or long before him, as Sulla, Marius, the two Lucullians, and Pompey [him]self, whose fame ascendeth up unto the heavens:

[but] it will appear that Caesar's **prowess** and deeds of arms, did excel them all together. For in less than ten years' war in Gaul he took [by storm] above eight hundred towns: he conquered three hundred several nations: and having before him in battle thirty hundred thousand soldiers, at sundry times he slew ten hundred thousand of them, and took as many more prisoners.

[He was so much master of the good-will and hearty service of his soldiers that those who in other expeditions were but ordinary men displayed a courage past defeating or withstanding when they went upon any danger where Caesar's glory was concerned.] And this appeareth plainly by the example of Acilius: who in a battle by sea before the city of Marselles, boarding one of his enemies' ships, one cut off his right hand with a sword, but yet he forsook not his target which he had in his left hand, but thrust it in his enemies' faces, and made them flee, so that he won their ship from them.

[Omitted for length: other stories of soldiers who demonstrated unusual dedication and courage. They are referred to in the following section.]

Part Three

Now Caesar's self did breed this noble courage and life in them. First, for that he gave them bountifully, and did honour them also, shewing thereby, that he did not heap up riches in the wars to maintain his life afterwards in wantonness and pleasure, but that he did keep it in store, honourably to reward their valiant service: and that by so much he thought himself rich, by how much he was liberal in rewarding of them that had deserved it.

Furthermore, they did not wonder so much at his valiantness in putting himself at every instant in such manifest danger, and in taking so extreme pains as he did, knowing that it was his greedy desire of honour that set him afire, and pricked him forward to do it: but that he always continued all labour and hardness, more than his body could bear, that filled them all with admiration. For, concerning the constitution of his body, he was lean, white, and soft skinned, and often **subject to headache, and otherwhile to the falling sickness**: (the which took him the first time, as it is reported, in Corduba, a city of Spain) but yet therefore yielded not to the disease of his body, to make it a cloak to cherish him withal, but contrarily, took the pains of war, as a medicine to cure his sick body fighting always with his disease, travelling continually, living **soberly**, and commonly lying abroad in the field. For the most nights he slept in his coach or litter, and thereby bestowed his rest, to make him always able to do something: and in the daytime, he would travel up and down the country to see towns, castles, and strong places.

He had always a secretary with him in his coach, who did still write as he went by the way, and a soldier behind him that carried his sword. He made such speed the first time he came from Rome, when he had his office: that in eight days, he came to the river of Rhone. He was so excellent a rider of horse from his youth, that holding his hands behind him, he would gallop his horse upon the spur.

In his wars in Gaul, he did further exercise himself to [dictate] letters as he rode by the way, and did occupy two secretaries at once with as much as they could write; and as Oppius writeth, more than two at a time. And it is reported, that Caesar was the first that devised friends might talk together **by writing ciphers in letters**, when he had no leisure to speak with them for his urgent business, and for the great distance besides from Rome.

How little account Caesar made of his diet, this example doth prove it. Caesar supping one night in Milan with his friend Valerius Leo, there was served **sparage** to his board, and oil of perfume put into it instead of salad oil. He simply ate it, and found no fault, blaming his friends that were offended: and told them, that it had been enough for them to have abstained to eat of that they misliked, and not to shame their friend, and how that he lacked good manner that found fault with his friend.

Narration and Discussion

Plutarch seems to jump quickly from Caesar's negative experience as consul to his career as "the wisest and most valiantest general." Should later success allow us to forget someone's earlier mistakes or misdeeds?

How did Caesar show himself an expert on time management as well as dinner-party etiquette?

Lesson Four

Introduction

"All Gaul is divided into three parts, one of which the Belgae inhabit, the Aquitani another, and those who in their own language are called Celts, in ours Gauls, the third. All these differ from each other in language, customs and laws." This is the famous beginning of *The Gallic Wars*, by Julius Caesar. The war for European control was a long, expensive gamble, but one that promised large returns.

Vocabulary

gave no place: refused to come second

break their strength: break down their fortification

void: empty, unoccupied

magistrates: elected officials

prorogue: extend

in choler: in a rage

People

Ariovistus: the leader of the Suebi tribe

Historic Occasions

58 B.C.: the beginning of the Gallic Wars

56 B.C: the meeting at Luca

55 B.C.: Caesar built a bridge across the Rhine, and invaded Britain

Reading

Part One

The first war that Caesar made with the Gauls, was with the Helvetians and Tigurinians, who having set fire of all their good cities, to the number of twelve, and four hundred villages besides, came to invade that part of Gaul which was subject to the Romans, as the Cimbri and Teutons had done before: unto whom for valiantness **they gave no place**, and [there] were also a great number of them (for they were three hundred thousand souls in all) whereof there were a hundred, fourscore, and ten thousand fighting men. Of those, it was not Caesar himself that overcame the Tigurinians, but [Titus] Labienus his lieutenant, that overthrew them by the river of Arax. But the Helvetians themselves came suddenly with their army to set upon him, as he was going towards a city of his confederates. Caesar perceiving that, made haste to get him some place of strength, and there did set his men in battle [ar]ray. When one brought him his horse to get up on which he used in battle, he said unto them: "When I have overcome mine enemies, I will then get up on him to follow the chase, but now let us give them charge."

Therewith he marched forward afoot, and gave charge: and there fought it out a long time, before he could make them flee that were in battle. But the greatest trouble he had, was to distress their camp, and to **break their strength** which they had made with their carts. For there, they that before had fled from the battle, did not only put themselves in force, and valiantly fought it out: but their wives and children also fighting for their lives to the death, were all slain, and the battle was scant ended at midnight.

Now if the act of this victory was famous, unto that he also added another as notable, or exceeding it. For of all the barbarous people that had escaped from [this] battle, he gathered together again above a hundred thousand of them, and compelled them to return home into their country which they had forsaken, and unto their towns also which they had burnt: because he feared the Germans would come over the river of Rhine, and occupy that country lying **void**.

Part Two

The second war he made was in defence of the Gauls against the Germans: although before, he himself had caused **Ariovistus**, their king, to be received for [an ally] of the Romans. Notwithstanding, they were grown very unquiet neighbours, and it appeared plainly, that having any occasion offered them to enlarge their territories, they would not content them with their own, but meant to invade and possess the rest of Gaul. Caesar, perceiving that some of his captains trembled for fear, but specially the young gentlemen of noble houses of Rome, who thought to have gone to the wars with him, as only for their pleasure and gain: he called them to council, and commanded them that were afraid, that they should depart home, and not put themselves in danger against their wills, [since] they had such womanish faint hearts to shrink when he had need of them. And for himself, he said, he would set upon the barbarous people, [even if] he had left him but the Tenth Legion only, saying that the enemies were no valianter than the Cimbri had been, nor that he [Caesar] was a captain inferior unto Marius.

This oration being made, the soldiers of the Tenth Legion sent their lieutenants unto him, to thank him for the good opinion he had of them: and the other legions also fell out with their captains, and all of them together followed him many days' journey with good will to serve him, until they came within two hundred furlongs of the camp of the enemies.

[A short description of the battle follows; the Romans were again victorious. After this, Caesar's army won a battle against the Nervians, "the stoutest warriors of all the Belgae."]

Part Three

For when Caesar had set his affairs at a stay in Gaul, on the other side of the Alps: he always used to lie about the river of Po in the wintertime, to give direction for the establishing of things at Rome, at his pleasure. For [instance], not only they that made suit for offices at Rome were chosen **magistrates**, by means of Caesar's money which he gave them, with the which, bribing the people, they bought their voices, and when they were in office, did all that they could to increase Caesar's power and greatness: but the greatest and chiefest men also of the nobility, [went to visit him at Luca, such as] Pompey; Crassus; Appius, praetor of Sardinia; and Nepos, proconsul in Spain. (Insomuch that there were at one time, six score sergeants carrying rods and axes before the magistrates: and above two hundred senators besides.) There [at this conference] they fell in consultation, and determined that Pompey and Crassus should again be chosen consuls the next year following.

Furthermore, they did appoint, that Caesar should have money again delivered him to pay his army, and besides, did **prorogue** the time of his government five years further. This was thought a very strange and an unreasonable matter unto wise men. For they themselves that had taken so much money of Caesar, persuaded the Senate to let him have money of the common treasure, as though he had had none before: yea to speak more plainly, they compelled the Senate unto it, sighing and lamenting to see the decrees they passed. Cato was not there then, for they had purposely sent him before into Cyprus. Howbeit Favonius that followed Cato's steps, when he saw that he could not prevail, nor withstand them: he went out of the Senate **in choler**, and cried out amongst the people, that it was a horrible shame. But no man did hearken to him: some for the reverence they bare unto Pompey and Crassus, and others favouring Caesar's proceedings, did put all their hope and trust in him: and therefore did quiet themselves, and stirred not.

Narration and Discussion

Why was the Roman Senate now more willing to grant Caesar money and other favours (even if the proposal came from his friends)?

Creative narration: Based on Plutarch's description, write (or give orally) Caesar's speech to his soldiers.

Lesson Five

Introduction

Caesar continued his military adventures in Gaul, but was somewhat disappointed by not finding much financial reward in fighting against barbarous peoples. At this time, he also received the news that his daughter Julia, Pompey's wife, had died in childbirth. When the Roman army had been divided into garrisons for the wintertime, and Caesar was in Italy, the Gauls rebelled against him again. But this time, fate seemed to favour the Romans.

Vocabulary

should the less esteem of them: would think they were weaker than they really were

plate and moveables: treasure, such as silver cups

caparison; caparison and furniture: decorative coverings for a horse

People

Ambiorix: the leader of the Eburones, an important tribe in northeastern Gaul

Cotta and Titurius: Lucius Aurunculeius Cotta and Quintus Titurius Sabinus

Quintus Cicero: Quintus Tullius Cicero; see introductory notes

Vercingentorix: the king of the Arverni; captured at the Battle of Alesia

Historic Occasions

53 B.C.: the death of Crassus; Gnaeus Domitius Calvinus was consul (see **Lesson Eight**)

52 B.C.: the Battle of Alesia

Reading

Part One

[Caesar's army was now grown very numerous, so that he was forced to disperse them into various camps for their winter quarters, and he having gone himself to Italy as he used to do, in his absence a general outbreak throughout the whole of Gaul commenced, and large armies marched about the country, and attacked the Roman quarters, and attempted to make themselves masters of the forts where they lay. The greatest and strongest party of the rebels, under the command of **Ambiorix**, cut off **Cotta and Titurius** with all their men, while a force sixty thousand strong besieged the legion under the command of **Quintus Cicero**, and had almost taken it by storm, the Roman soldiers being all wounded, and having quite spent themselves by a defence beyond their natural strength]

These news being come to Caesar, who was far from thence at that time, he returned with all possible speed, and levying seven thousand soldiers, made haste to help Cicero that was in such distress. The Gauls that did besiege Cicero, understanding of Caesar's coming, raised their siege to go and meet him: making account that he was but a handful in their hands, they were so few. Caesar, to deceive them, still drew back, and made as though he fled from them, lodging in places meet for a captain that had but a few, to fight with a great number of his enemies, and commanded his men in no wise to stir out to skirmish with them, but compelled them to raise up the ramparts of his camp, and to fortify the gates, as men that were afraid, because the enemies **should the less esteem of them**: until that at length he took opportunity, by their disorderly coming, to assail the trenches of his camp (they were grown to such a presumptuous boldness and bravery); and then sallying out upon them, he put them all to flight with slaughter of a great number of them.

This did suppress all the rebellions of the Gauls in those parts, and furthermore, he himself in person went in the midst of winter thither, where[ever] he heard they did rebel: for that there was come a new supply out of Italy of three whole legions: of the which, two of them Pompey lent him, and the other legion, he himself had levied in Gaul about the river of Po.

[But in a while the seeds of war, which had long since been secretly sown and scattered by the most powerful men in those warlike nations, broke forth into the greatest and most dangerous war that was in those parts.] For everywhere they levied multitudes of men, and great riches besides, to fortify their strongholds. Furthermore the country where they rose, was very ill to come unto, and specially at that time being winter, when the rivers were frozen, the woods and forests covered with snow, the meadows drowned with floods, and the fields so deep of snow, that no ways were to be found, neither the marshes nor rivers to be discerned, all was so overflown and drowned with water: all which troubles together were enough (as they thought) to keep Caesar from setting upon the rebels.

Many nations of the Gauls were of this conspiracy, but two of the chiefest were the Arvernians and Carnutes: who had chosen **Vercingentorix** for their lieutenant general, whose father the Gauls before had put to death, because they thought he [the father] aspired to make himself king. [Vercingentorix having disposed his army in several bodies, and set officers over them, drew over to him all the country round about as far as those that lie upon the Arar, and having intelligence of the opposition which Caesar now experienced at Rome, thought to engage all Gaul in the war.] So that if he had but tarried a little longer, until Caesar had entered into his civil wars: he [would have] put all Italy in as great fear and danger, as it was when the Cimbri did come and invade it.

[But Caesar, who above all men was gifted with the faculty of making the right use of everything in war, and most especially of seizing the right moment]: so soon as he understood the news of the rebellion, he departed with speed, and returned back the selfsame way which he had gone, making the barbarous people know, that they should deal with an army invincible, and which they could not possibly withstand, considering the great speed he had made with the same, in so sharp and hard a winter. For where they would not possibly have believed, that a post or courier could have come in so short a time from the place where he was, unto them: they wondered when they saw him burning and destroying the country, the towns and strong forts where he came with his army, taking all to mercy that yielded unto him: until such time as the Hedvi took arms against him, who before were wont to be called the brethren of the Romans, and were greatly honoured of them. Wherefore Caesar's men, when they understood that they had joined with the rebels, they were marvellous sorry, and half discouraged.

Part Two

Thereupon Caesar, departing from those parts, went through the country of the Lingones, to enter the country of the Burgonians, who were confederates of the Romans, and the nearest unto Italy on that side, in respect of all the rest of Gaul. Thither the enemies came to set upon him, and to environ him of all sides, with an infinite number of thousands of fighting men. Caesar on the other side tarried their coming, and fighting with them a long time, he made them so afraid of him, that at length he overcame the barbarous people. But at the first, it seemeth notwithstanding, that he had received some overthrow: for the Arvernians shewed a sword hanged up in one of their temples, which they said they had won from Caesar. Insomuch as Caesar [him]self coming that way by occasion, saw it, and fell a-laughing at it. But some of his friends going about to take it away, he would not suffer them, but bade them let it alone, and touch it not, for it was a holy thing.

Notwithstanding, such as at the first had saved themselves by fleeing, the most of them were gotten with their king into the city of Alesia, the which Caesar went and besieged, although it seemed [impregnable], both for the height of the walls, as also for the multitude of soldiers they had to defend it. But now, during this siege, he fell into a marvellous great danger without, almost incredible. For an army of three hundred thousand fighting men of the best men that were among all the nations of the Gauls, came against him, being at the siege of Alesia, besides them that were within the city, which amounted to the number of three score and ten thousand fighting men at the least: so that perceiving he was shut in betwixt two so great armies, he was driven to fortify himself with two walls, the one against them of the city, and the other against them without. For if those two armies had joined together, Caesar [would have] been utterly undone. And therefore this siege of Alesia, and the battle he won before it, did deservedly win him more honour and fame, than any other. For there, in that instant and extreme danger, he shewed more valiantness and wisdom than he did in any battle he fought before.

But what a wonderful thing was this? that they of the city never heard anything of them that came to aid them, until Caesar had overcome them: and furthermore, that the Romans themselves which kept watch upon the wall that was built against the city, knew also no more of it than they, but when it was done, and that they heard the cries and lamentations of men and women in Alesia, when they perceived on the other side of the city such a number of glistering shields of gold and silver, such store of bloody corselets and armours, such a deal of **plate and moveables**, and such a number of tents and pavilions after the fashion of the Gauls, which the Romans had gotten of their spoils in their camp. [So soon did so vast an army dissolve and vanish like a ghost or dream, the greatest part of them being killed upon the spot.]

Furthermore, after they within the city of Alesia had done great hurt to Caesar, and themselves also: in the end, they all yielded themselves. And Vercingentorix (he that was their king and captain in all this war) went out of the gates excellently well armed, and his horse furnished with rich **caparis**on accordingly, and rode round about Caesar, who sat in his chair of estate. Then lighting from his horse, he took off his **caparison and furniture**, and unarmed himself, and laid all on the ground, and went and sat down at Caesar's feet, and said never a word. So Caesar at length committed him as a prisoner taken in the wars, to lead him afterwards in his triumph at Rome.

Narration and Discussion

What skills as a general did Caesar demonstrate during these battles?

Lesson Six

Introduction

The struggle for power in Rome was becoming ugly. Some wanted to bring back the authority of a king or a dictator, to end the chaos; or at least elect a powerful consul to do the same thing, and the obvious choice for that was Pompey. He was elected for a third (non-consecutive) term as consul in 52 B.C., the same year as Caesar's victory at Alesia.

Vocabulary

the commonwealth: Rome and its provinces and colonies

covertly: secretly

lay all the irons in the fire he could: try everything he could think of

prorogue: extend

Marcellus and Lentulus...withstood them: they were both running against Caesar for consul, and they spoke out against his representatives

magistrates: elected officials

basilica: a Roman building used as a court of justice

send Caesar a successor [as governor]: send a replacement and force him to return to Rome

silver drachmas: coins

as private persons: out of office, without authority

Ariminum: the modern city of Rimini

stayed: stopped

People

Cato: Cato the Younger (see introductory notes)

Marcellus: Marcus Claudius Marcellus, consul in 51 B.C., and the brother of **Marcellus (Maior)**

Paul the consul: Lucius Aemilius Lepidus Paullus, consul in 50 B.C. along with Gaius Claudius Marcellus, called **Marcellus (Minor)**

Lentulus: Lucius Cornelius Lentulus Crus, consul in 49 B.C., along with **Marcellus (Maior)**, a cousin of the previous consul

Curio: an **orator** (see introductory note) and statesman

Antonius: Marcus Antonius, or Mark Antony

Asinius Pollio: Gaius Asinius Pollio, a Roman orator and historian

Historic Occasions

50 B.C.: The Senate, led by Pompey, ordered Caesar to disband his army and return to Rome because his term as governor had ended

January, 49 B.C.: Caesar crossed the Rubicon into Italy, an act of defiance which began a civil war

Reading

Part One

[So that after having many times stained the place of election with blood of men killed upon the spot, they left the city at last without a government at all, to be carried about like a ship without a pilot to steer her; while all who had any wisdom could only be thankful if a course of such wild and stormy disorder and madness might end no worse than in a monarchy.] Furthermore, there were many that were not afraid to speak it openly, that there was no other help to remedy the troubles of **the commonwealth**, but by the authority of one man only, that should command them all: and that this medicine must be ministered by the hands of him that was the gentlest physician, meaning, **covertly**, Pompey. Now Pompey used many fine speeches, making semblance as though he would [have] none of it, and yet cunningly underhand did **lay all the irons in the fire he could**, to bring it to pass, that he might be chosen dictator. **Cato** finding the mark he shot at, and fearing lest in the end the people should be compelled to make him dictator: he persuaded the Senate rather to make him [Pompey] sole consul, that contenting himself with that more just and lawful government, he should not covet the other [which was] unlawful.

The Senate following his [Cato's] counsel, did not only make him [Pompey] consul, but further did **prorogue** his government of the provinces he [governed]. For he had two provinces, all Spain, and Africa, which he governed by his lieutenants: and further, he received yearly of the common treasure to pay his soldiers a thousand talents.

Hereupon Caesar took occasion also to send his men to make suit in his name for the consulship, and also to have the government of his [own] provinces **prorogued**. Pompey at the first held his peace.

But **Marcellus and Lentulus** (that otherwise hated Caesar) **withstood them** [Caesar's representatives], and to shame and dishonour him, had much needless speech in matters of weight. [For they took away the privilege of Roman citizens from the people of New Comum, who were a colony that Caesar had lately planted in Gaul.] And moreover, when [**Marcus Claudius Marcellus**] was consul, he made one of the senators in that city to be whipped with rods, who came to Rome about those matters: and said [that] he gave him those marks, that he should know he was no Roman citizen, and bade him go his way, and tell Caesar of it.

After [**Marcus Claudius Marcellus'**] consulship, Caesar setting open his coffers of the treasure he had gotten among the Gauls, did frankly give it out amongst the **magistrates** at Rome, without restraint or spare. First, he set **Curio**, the tribune, clear out of debt: and gave also unto **Paul the consul**, a thousand five hundred talents, with which money he built that notable palace by the marketplace, called Paul's **Basilica**, in the place of Fulvius' Basilica. Then Pompey, being afraid of this practice, began openly to procure, both by himself and his friends, that they should **send Caesar a successor [as governor]**; moreover, he sent unto Caesar for [the return of] his two legions of men of war which he had lent him, for the conquest of Gaul. Caesar sent him them again, and gave every private soldier two hundred and fifty **silver drachmas**.

Notwithstanding, the requests that Caesar propounded carried great semblance of reason with them. For he said, that he was contented to lay down arms, so that Pompey did the like: and that both of them **as private persons** should come and make suit of their citizens to obtain honourable recompense: declaring unto them, that taking arms from him, and granting them unto Pompey, they did wrongfully accuse him in going about to make himself a tyrant, and in the meantime to grant the other [man the] means to be a tyrant.

Curio making these offers and persuasions openly before the people, in the name of Caesar: he was heard with great rejoicing and clapping of hands, and there were some that cast flowers and nosegays upon him when he went his way, as they commonly used to do for [successful wrestlers, crowned with flowers]. Then **Antonius**, one of the tribunes, brought a letter sent from Caesar, and made it openly to be read in despite of the consuls. But Scipio in the Senate, Pompey's father-in-law, made this motion: that if Caesar did not dismiss his army by a certain day appointed him, the Romans should proclaim him an enemy unto Rome.

After that, there came other letters from Caesar, which seemed much more reasonable: in the which he requested that they would grant him Gaul, that lieth between the Mountains of the Alps and Italy, and Illyria, with two legions only, and then that he would request nothing else, until he made suit for the second consulship.

Part Two

Now at that time, Caesar had not in all about him above five thousand footmen, and three thousand horsemen: for the rest of his army, he left on the other side of the mountains, to be brought after him by his lieutenants. So, considering that for the execution of his enterprise, he should not need so many men of war at the first, but rather suddenly stealing upon them, [so to astound his enemies with the boldness of it], taking benefit of the opportunity of time, because he should more easily make his enemies afraid of him, coming so suddenly when they looked not for him, than he should otherwise distress them, assailing them with his whole army, in giving them leisure to provide further for him: he commanded his captains and lieutenants to go before, without any other armour than their swords, to take the city of **Ariminum** (a great city of Gaul, being the first city men come to, when they come out of Gaul), with as little bloodshed and tumult, as they could possibl[y].

Then committing that force and army he had with him, unto Hortensius, one of his friends: he remained a whole day together, openly in the sight of every man, [as a stander-by and spectator of the gladiators, who exercised before him]. At night he went into his lodging, and bathing his body a little, came afterwards into the hall amongst them, and made merry with them awhile, whom he had bidden to supper. Then when it was well forward night, and very dark, he rose from the table, and prayed his company to be merry, and no man to stir, for he would straight come to them again: howbeit he had secretly before commanded a few of his trustiest friends to follow him, not altogether, but some one way, and some another way. He himself in the meantime took a coach he had hired, and made as though he would have gone some other way at the first, but suddenly he turned back again towards the city of **Ariminum**.

When he was come unto the little river of Rubicon, which divideth Gaul on this side the Alps from Italy: he stayed upon a sudden.

For, the nearer he came to execute his purpose, the more remorse he had in his conscience, to think what an enterprise he took in hand: and his thoughts also fell out more doubtful, when he entered into consideration of the desperateness of his attempt. So he fell into many thoughts with himself, and spake never a word, wav[er]ing sometime one way, sometime another way [Dryden: *while he revolved with himself*], and often times changed his determination, contrary to himself. So did he talk much also with his friends he had with him, amongst whom was **Asinius Pollio**, telling them what mischiefs the beginning of this passage over that river would breed in the world, and how much their posterity and them that lived after them, would speak of it in time to come.

But at length, casting from him with a noble courage, all those perilous thoughts to come, and speaking these words which valiant men commonly say, that attempt dangerous and desperate enterprises, "A desperate man feareth no danger, come on" [Dryden: *"The die is cast", which can also be translated "Let the die be cast"*]: he passed over the river, and when he was come over, he ran with his coach and never **stayed**, so that before daylight he was within the city of **Ariminum**, and took it.

Narration and Discussion

Why did the Romans decide against electing a dictator?

In **Part One**, Plutarch says that Caesar put his name forward for a second term as consul. It sounds at first as if this happened during the year (52 B.C.) that Pompey was consul, but it appears to have taken place during the elections of 50 B.C., which would determine the consuls for 49 B.C. What might Caesar's intention have been? Why did he lose the race to Marcellus and Lentulus?

"To cross the Rubicon" is an expression we use to mean "the point of no return." What did it mean for Julius Caesar?

Lesson Seven

Introduction

The reaction to Caesar's taking of the city of Ariminium was immediate and violent. Hordes of people from outside Rome arrived in the city, fearing their own homes would be attacked. Some people blamed Pompey for not co-operating more fully with Caesar; others blamed him for not controlling him. The general panic led to the fleeing of both the consuls and many of the senators.

Vocabulary

Corfinium: a fortified city on the eastern side of the Apennines

clemency: mercy

tarried not: did not wait for

fled into the city of Brundisium: Pompey was trying to get to Epirus, to raise support for a blockade of Italy.

Dyrrhachium: the capital of the province of Epirus, where a battle was fought between Caesar's and Pompey's forces

they were words of course, to colour his purpose withal: it was just a lot of talk, and not the truth

the temple of Saturn: the public treasury

pulpit, pulpit for orations: the Rostra, or speakers' platform

bigly: loudly

victuals: food, supplies

to treat of peace: to discuss a peace treaty or agreement

follow the wars: renew his pursuit of Pompey

the Sea Ionium: the Ionian Sea, between Italy and Greece

People

Domitius: Lucius Domitius Ahenobarbus, an enemy of Caesar; not to be confused with Gnaeus Domitius Calvinus, who remained loyal to Caesar

Servilius Isauricus: co-consul with Caesar for 48 B.C.

Historic Occasions

48 B.C.: Caesar became consul for the second time, but immediately took an army to Greece to hunt down Pompey

Reading

Part One

There were some [Romans] also, that always loved Caesar, whose wits were then so troubled and beside themselves, with the fear they had conceived: that they also fled, and followed the stream of this tumult, without manifest cause or necessity. But above all things, it was a lamentable sight to see the city itself, that in this fear and trouble was left at all adventure, as a ship tossed in storm of sea, forsaken of her pilots, and despairing of her safety. Their departure being thus miserable, yet men esteemed their [own] banishment (for the love they bare unto Pompey) to be their natural country and reckoned Rome no better than Caesar's camp.

At that time also Labienus, who was one of Caesar's greatest friends, and [who] had been always used as his lieutenant in the wars of Gaul, and had valiantly fought in his cause: he likewise forsook him then, and fled unto Pompey. But Caesar sent his money and carriage after him, and then went and encamped before the city of **Corfinium**, which **Domitius** kept, with thirty cohorts or ensigns.

When Domitius saw he was besieged, he straight thought himself but undone, and despairing of his success, he bade a physician, a slave of his, give him poison. The physician gave him a drink, which he drank, thinking to have died. But shortly after, Domitius hearing them report what **clemency** and wonderful courtesy Caesar used unto them he took: [he] repented him then that he had drunk this drink, and began to lament and bewail his desperate resolution taken to die. The physician did comfort him again, and told him, that he had taken a drink, only to make him sleep, but not to destroy him. Then Domitius rejoiced, and went straight and yielded himself unto Caesar: who gave him his life, but he notwithstanding stole away immediately, and fled unto Pompey.

When these news were brought to Rome, they did marvellously rejoice and comfort them that still remained there: and moreover there were [some] of them that had forsaken Rome, which returned thither again. In the meantime, Caesar did put all Domitius' men in pay, and he did the like through all the cities, where he had taken any captains that levied men for Pompey.

Now Caesar having assembled a great and dreadful power together, went straight where he thought to find Pompey himself. But Pompey **tarried not** his coming, but **fled into the city of Brundisium**, from whence he had sent the two consuls before, with that army he had, unto **Dyrrhachium**: and he himself also went [to Dyrrhachium] afterwards, when he understood that Caesar was come, as you shall hear more amply hereafter in his *Life*. Caesar lacked no goodwill to follow him, but wanting ships to take the seas, he returned forthwith to Rome.

So that in less than threescore days, he was lord of all Italy, without any bloodshed. When he was come to Rome, and found it much quieter than he looked for, and many senators there also: he courteously entreated them, and prayed them to send unto Pompey, to pacify all matters between them, upon reasonable conditions. But no man did attempt it, either because they feared Pompey for that they had forsaken him, or else for that they thought Caesar meant not as he spake, but that **they were words of course, to colour his purpose withal**.

And when Metellus also, one of the tribunes, would not suffer him to take any of the common treasure out of **the temple of Saturn**, but told him that it was against the law:

> "Tush," said he, "time of war and law are two things.
> If this that I do," quoth he, "do offend thee, then get
> thee hence for this time: for war can not abide this
> frank and bold speech. But when wars are done, and
> that we are all quiet again, then thou shalt speak in
> **the pulpit** what thou wilt: and yet I do tell thee this

of favour, impairing so much my right, for thou art mine, both thou and all them that have risen against me, and whom I have in my hands."

When he had spoken thus unto Metellus, he went to the temple door where the treasure lay: and finding no keys there, he caused smiths to be sent for, and made them break open the locks. Metellus thereupon began again to withstand him, and certain men that stood by praised him in his doing: but Caesar at length speaking **bigly** to him, threatened him he would kill him presently, if he troubled him any more: and told him furthermore, "Young man," quoth he, "thou knowest it is harder for me to tell it thee, than to do it." That word made Metellus quake for fear, that he got him away roundly: and ever after that, Caesar had all at his commandment for the wars.

Part Two

From thence he went into Spain, to make war with Lucius Afranius and Marcus Petreius, Pompey's lieutenants: first to get their armies and provinces into his hands which they governed, [and then] afterwards he might follow Pompey the better, leaving never an enemy behind him. In this journey he was oftentimes himself in danger, through the ambushes that were laid for him in divers strange sorts and places, and likely also to have lost all his army for lack of **victuals**. All this notwithstanding, he never left following of Pompey's lieutenants, provoking them to battle, and entrenching them in: until he had gotten their camp and armies into his hands [*at the Battle of Ilerda*], albeit that the lieutenants themselves fled unto Pompey.

When Caesar returned again to Rome [*December, 49 B.C.*], Piso his father-in-law gave him counsel to send ambassadors unto Pompey, **to treat of peace**. But **Isauricus**, to flatter Caesar, was against it. Caesar being then created dictator by the Senate, called home again all the banished men, and restored their children to honour, whose fathers before had been slain in Sulla's time: [and he relieved the debtors by an act remitting some part of the interest on their debts], and besides, did make some such other ordinances as those, but very few. For he was dictator but eleven days only, and then did yield it up of himself, and made himself consul, with **Servilius Isauricus**, and after that [he] determined to **follow the wars**.

[He marched so fast that he left all his army behind him], and went himself before with six hundred horse, and five legions only of footmen, in the winter quarter, about the month of January, which after the Athenians, is called Posideon. Then having passed over **the Sea Ionium**, and landed his men, he won the cities of Oricum and Apollonia. Then he sent his ships back again unto Brundisium, to transport the rest of his soldiers that could not come with that speed he did. They as they came by the way, (like men whose strength of body was decayed) being wearied with so many sundry battles as they had fought with their enemies: complained of Caesar in this sort.

> "To what end and purpose doth this man hale us
> after him, up and down the world, using us like
> slaves and drudges? It is not our armour, but our
> bodies that bear the blows away: and what, shall we
> never be without our harness of our backs, and our
> shields on our arms? Should not Caesar think, at
> the least when he seeth our blood and wounds, that
> we are all mortal men, and that we feel the misery
> and pains that other men do feel? And now even in
> the dead of winter, he putteth us unto the mercy of
> the sea and tempest, yea which the gods themselves
> can not withstand: as if he fled before his enemies,
> and pursued them not."

Thus spending time with this talk, the soldiers still marching on, by small journeys, [they] came at length unto the city of Brundisium. But when they were come, and found that Caesar had already passed over the sea, then they straight changed their complaints and minds. For they blamed themselves, and took on also with their captains, because they had not made them make more haste in marching: and sitting upon the rocks and cliffs of the sea, they looked over the main sea, towards the realm of Epirus, to see if they could discern the ships returning back, to transport them over.

Narration and Discussion

"Time of war and law are two things." Do you agree?

Why did the soldiers' discovery that Caesar had arrived in Greece ahead of them give them new motivation to continue?

Lesson Eight

Introduction

Caesar and Antonius, in spite of difficulty and foot-dragging by battle-weary soldiers, gathered an army together in Epirus to fight Pompey's Republican resistance troops. They lost the battle, but not the war, because, according to Caesar, Pompey had victory in his hands but did not seem to know what to do with it. Both armies moved on to Thessaly, where a final showdown was in the air.

Vocabulary

who was passingly well lodged, for victualing of his camp: who was in a fairly good position to keep his army supplied

hard to the trenches: almost up to the boundary

saving once only: A traitor in Caesar's army informed Pompey of a weak spot in their fortifications. Pompey took advantage of this and broke through, forcing Caesar's army to retreat (although, as Plutarch says, he decided not to follow them).

straited with victuals: frustrated by lack of supplies

the infection of the pestilence: there had been illness in Caesar's camp

dancing, masquing, and playing the Baccherians: what we would call partying

the chief bishopric: the office of *Pontifex Maximus*. They argued over which one would get the position, once they had defeated Caesar.

devise some fetch: come up with some ruse or trick

environ: surround

People

Spinther: Publius Cornelius Lentulus, nicknamed Spinther

Cornificius: Plutarch says Corfinius here, but that may be an error

[Gnaeius] Domitius Calvinus: a general, senator, and former consul
who was loyal to Caesar and (later) to Octavius (Caesar Augustus).
After the Battle of Pharsalus, he was made the Governor of Asia.

Historic Occasions

July, 48 B.C.: the Battle of Dyrrhachium

August, 48 B.C.: the Battle of Pharsalus

Reading

Part One

Then Caesar finding himself strong enough, went and offered
Pompey battle, **who was passingly well lodged, for victualing of
his camp** both by sea and land. Caesar on the other side, who had
no great plenty of victuals at the first, was in a very hard case:
insomuch as his men gathered roots, and mingled them with milk,
and ate them. Furthermore, they did make bread of it also, and [and
advancing up to the enemy's outposts, would throw these loaves [at
the guards], telling them, that as long as the earth produced such
roots they would not give up blockading Pompey. [But Pompey took
what care he could that neither the loaves nor the words should reach
his men, who were out of heart and despondent through terror at the
fierceness and hardihood of their enemies, whom they looked upon
as a sort of wild beasts.]

Caesar's men did daily skirmish **hard to the trenches** of
Pompey's camp, in the which Caesar had ever the better, **saving
once only**, at what time his men fled with such fear, that all his camp
that day was in great hazard to have been cast away. For Pompey
came on with his battle upon them, and they were not able to abide
it, but were fought with, and driven into their camp, and their
trenches were filled with dead bodies, which were slain within the
very gate and bulwarks of their camp, they were so valiantly pursued.
Caesar stood before them that fled, to make them to turn head again:
but he could not prevail. For when he would have taken the ensigns
to have stayed them, the ensign bearers threw them down on the
ground: so that the enemies took thirty-two of them, and Caesar

[him]self also escaped hardly with life. For striking a great big soldier that fled by him, commanding him to stay, and turn his face to his enemy: the soldier being afraid, lift[ed] up his sword to strike at Caesar. But one of Caesar's pages preventing him, gave him such a blow with his sword, that he struck off his shoulder. [Caesar's affairs were so desperate at that time that when Pompey, either through over-cautiousness or his ill fortune, did not give the finishing stroke to that great success, but retreated after he had driven the routed enemy within their camp; Caesar, upon seeing his withdrawal, said to his friends, "The victory today had been on the enemies' side, if they had had a general who knew how to gain it."]

So when he was come to his lodging, he went to bed, and that night troubled him more than any night that ever he had. For still his mind ran with great sorrow of the foul fault he had committed in leading of his army. [For when he had a fertile country before him, and all the wealthy cities of Macedonia and Thessaly, he had neglected to carry the war thither, and had sat down by the seaside, where his enemies had such a powerful fleet, so that he was, in fact, rather besieged by the want of necessaries, than besieging others with his arms.] Thus, fretting and chafing to see himself so **straited with victuals**, and to think of his ill luck, he raised his camp, intending to go set upon Scipio, [who lay in Macedonia], making account, that either he should draw Pompey to battle against his will, when he had not the sea at his back to furnish him with plenty of victuals: or else that he should easily overcome Scipio, finding him alone, unless he were aided.

Part Two

Then was Caesar, at the first, marvellously perplexed, and troubled by the way: because he found none that would give him any victuals, being despised of every man, for the late loss and overthrow he had received. But after he had taken the city of Gomphi in Thessaly, he did not only meet with plenty of victuals to relieve his army: but he strangely also did rid them of their disease. For the soldiers meeting with plenty of wine, drinking hard, and making merry: drove away **the infection of the pestilence**. For they disposed themselves unto **dancing, masquing, and playing the Baccherians** by the way: insomuch that drinking drunk, they overcame their disease, and made

41

their bodies new again.

[Pompey would have preferred to avoid engaging Caesar's army, because he knew that the enemy was short on supplies and might have to back down for that reason. However, his own men provoked him to follow Caesar and to fight.]

When they both came into the country of Pharsalus, and both camps lay before the other: Pompey returned again to his former determination [to avoid fighting], and the rather, because he had ill signs and tokens of misfortune in his sleep. [But] they that were about him grew to such boldness and security, assuring themselves of victory: that Domitius, **Spinther**, and Scipio, in a bravery, contended between themselves for **the chief bishopric** which Caesar had. [And many sent to Rome to take houses fit to accommodate consuls and praetors, as being sure of entering upon those offices as soon as the battle was over.] But besides those, the young gentlemen and Roman knights were marvellous desirous to fight, that were bravely mounted, and armed with glistering gilt armours, their horses fat and very finely kept, and themselves goodly young men, to the number of seven thousand, where the gentlemen of Caesar's side were but one thousand only. The number of his footmen also were much after the same reckoning; for he had five, and Pompey's forty thousand, against two and twenty thousand.

Wherefore Caesar called his soldiers together, and told them how **Cornificius** was at hand, who brought two whole legions, and that he had fifteen ensigns led by Calenus, the which he made to stay about Megara and Athens. Then he asked them if they would tarry for that aid or not, or whether they would rather themselves alone venture battle. The soldiers cried out to him, and prayed him not to defer battle, but rather to **devise some fetch** to make the enemy fight as soon as he could. Then as he sacrificed unto the gods, for the purifying of his army: the first beast was no sooner sacrificed, but his soothsayer assured him that he should fight within three days. Caesar asked him again, if he saw in the sacrifices, any lucky sign, or token of good luck. The soothsayer answered, "For that, thou shalt answer thyself, better than I can do: for the gods do promise us a marvellous great change, and alteration of things that are now, unto another clean contrary. For if thou beest well now, dost thou think to have worse fortune hereafter? and if thou be ill, assure thyself thou shalt have better."

The night before the battle, as he went about midnight to visit the watch, [there was a light seen in the heavens, very bright and flaming, which seemed to pass over Caesar's camp and fall into Pompey's]. In the morning also, when they relieved the watch, they heard a false alarm in the enemies' camp, without any apparent cause: which they commonly call a sudden fear that makes men besides themselves. This notwithstanding, Caesar thought not to fight that day, but was determined to have raised his camp from thence, and to have gone towards the city of Scotusa: and his tents in his camp were already overthrown when his scouts came in with great speed, to bring him news that his enemies were preparing themselves to fight.

Then he was very glad, and after he had made his prayers unto the gods to help him that day, he set his men in battle [ar]ray, and divided them into three squadrons: giving the middle battle unto **Domitius Calvinus**, and the left wing unto Antonius, and placed himself in the right wing, choosing his place to fight in the tenth legion. But seeing that against [his forces] his enemies had set all their horsemen: he was half afraid when he saw the great number of them, and so brave besides. Wherefore he [privately] made six ensigns to come from the rearward of his battle, whom he had laid as an ambush behind his right wing, having first appointed his soldiers what they should do, when the horsemen of the enemies came to give them charge.

On the other side, Pompey placed himself in the right wing of his battle, gave the left wing unto Domitius [*the other Domitius*], and the middle battle unto Scipio, his father-in-law.

Now all [Pompey's] knights (as we have told you before) were placed in the left wing, of purpose to **environ** Caesar's right wing behind, and to give their hottest charge there, where the general of their enemies was: making their account, that there was no squadron of footmen how thick soever they were, that could receive the charge of so great a troop of horsemen, [but that they must necessarily be broken and shattered all to pieces upon the onset of so immense a force of cavalry].

[Pompey's horsemen were ambushed by Caesar's ensigns, and began to flee.]

Pompey, seeing his horsemen from the other wing of his battle so scattered and dispersed, fleeing away: forgot that he was any more

Pompey the Great which he had been before, but rather was like a man whose wits the gods had taken from him, being afraid and amazed with the slaughter sent from above, and so retired into his tent speaking never a word, and sat there to see the end of this battle. Until at length all his army being overthrown, and put to flight, the enemies came, and got up upon the ramparts and defence of his camp, and fought hand to hand with them that stood to defend the same. Then as a man come to himself again, he spake but this only word: "What, even into our camp?" So in haste, casting off his coat [of] armour and apparel of a general, he shifted him, and put on such [clothing], as became his miserable fortune, and so stole out of his camp. Furthermore, what he did after this overthrow, and how he had put himself into the hands of the Egyptians, by whom he was miserably slain: we have set it forth at large in his *Life*.

Narration and Discussion

Why did Caesar decide to change his strategy after the defeat at the Battle of Dyrrhachium?

If we cannot credit "drinking drunk" with healing the soldiers' disease, what might have been the cause of their return to health and better spirits?

Creative Narration: After the Battle of Dyrrhachium, Caesar moved most of his troops into the region of Thessaly (in Greece), and took the city of Gomphi. Another source says that at this time he reconnected with Domitius Calvinus, during the time that his men were taking their "holiday." Imagine (write or act out) a conversation that might have taken place between them at that point.

What were some of the good and not-so-good decisions that Caesar and Pompey made during the Battle of Pharsalus?

Lesson Nine

Introduction

After the Battle of Pharsalus, a great deal happened quickly for

Caesar. He was appointed dictator of Rome, and kept that title just long enough to oversee his own election as consul; he then left for Egypt to look for Pompey. He arrived there just after Pompey's death, and had his murderers executed At this point Caesar might have returned to Rome, but he became involved in Egyptian politics, and also with the pharaoh's sister, Cleopatra. He also fought with Pharnaces, the king of Pontus.

Vocabulary

vaunt: boast

fardel: package, bundle

that notable library of Alexandria: Plutarch claims that the library was burned at this time, but other sources say that the fire did not much damage the library, and that it was destroyed later.

tower of Phar: the Pharos or Lighthouse of Alexandria

But for the king...: King Ptolemy XIII is assumed to have drowned during the battle.

Cleopatra Queen of Egypt: she was co-ruler with another brother, Ptolemy XIV

People

Pothinus the eunuch: a high-ranking servant of King Ptolemy XIII, and also his regent since Ptolemy was very young

Achillas: a guardian of King Ptolemy, and one of the murderers of Pompey

Caesarion: Caesar's son (it is assumed), and the last pharaoh of Egypt.

Historic Occasions

48/47 B.C.: Caesar's adventures in Egypt, including the Siege of Alexandria

47 B.C.: the Battle of Zela, against King Pharnaces of Pontus

Reading

Part One

As for [the footsoldiers of Pompey] that were taken prisoners, Caesar did put many of them amongst his legions, and did pardon also many men of estimation; among whom Brutus was one, that afterwards slew Caesar himself; and it is reported, that Caesar was very sorry for him, when he could not immediately be found after the battle, and that he rejoiced again, when he knew he was alive, and that he came to yield himself unto him. Caesar [kindly treated] all Pompey's friends and familiars who, wandering up and down the country, were taken of the king of Egypt; and won them all to be at his commandment. Continuing these courtesies, he wrote unto his friends at Rome, that the greatest pleasure he took of his victory was that he daily saved the lives of some of his countrymen that bare arms against him.

And for the war he made in Alexandria, some say he needed not have done it, but that he willingly did it for the love of Cleopatra: wherein he won little honour, and besides did put his person in great danger. Others do lay the fault upon the king of Egypt's ministers, but specially on **Pothinus the eunuch**, who bearing the greatest sway of all the king's servants, after he had caused Pompey to be slain, and driven Cleopatra from the court, secretly laid wait all the ways he could, how he might likewise kill Caesar.

Wherefore Caesar, hearing an inkling of it, began thenceforth to spend all the night long in feasting and banqueting, that his person might be in the better safety. But besides all this, Pothinus spake many things openly not to be borne, only to shame Caesar, and to stir up the people to envy him. For he made his soldiers have the worst and oldest wheat that could be gotten: then if they did complain of it, he told them, they must be contented, seeing they ate at another man's cost. [He also ordered that his table should be served with wooden and earthen dishes, and said Caesar had carried off all the gold and silver plate, under pretence of arrears of debt.]

Caesar secretly sent for Cleopatra, which was in the country, to come unto him. She only taking Apollodorus Sicilian of all her friends, took a little boat, and went away with him in it in the night, and came and landed hard by the foot of the castle. Then having no other mean[s] to come into the court without being known, she laid herself down upon a mattress or flockbed, which Apollodorus her friend tied and bound up together like a bundle with a great leather thong, and so took her up on his back, and brought her thus hampered in this **fardel** unto Caesar, in at the castle gate. This was the first occasion, (as it is reported) that made Caesar to love her: but afterwards, when he saw her sweet conversation and pleasant entertainment, he fell then in further liking with her, and did reconcile her again unto her brother the king, with condition, that they two jointly should reign together.

Part Two

Upon this new reconciliation, a great feast being prepared, a slave of Caesar's that was his barber, the fearfullest wretch that lived, still busily prying and listening abroad in every corner, being mistrustful by nature: found that Pothinus and **Achillas** did lie in wait to kill his master Caesar. This being proved unto Caesar, he did set such sure watch about the hall, where the feast was made, that in fine, he slew Pothinus himself. Achillas on the other side, saved himself, and fled unto the king's camp, where he raised a marvellous dangerous and difficult war for Caesar: because he having then but a few men about him as he had, he was to fight against a great and strong city.

The first danger he fell into, was for the lack of water he had: for that his enemies had stopped the mouth of the pipes, which conveyed the water unto the castle. The second danger he had, was, that seeing his enemies came to take his ships from him, he was driven to repulse that danger with fire [*by setting fire to his own ships*], the which burnt the arsenal where the ships lay, and **that notable library of Alexandria** withal. The third danger was in the battle by sea, that was fought by the **tower of Phar**: where meaning to help his men that fought by sea, he leapt from the pier, into a boat. Then the Egyptians made towards him with their oars, on every side: but he leaping into the sea, with great hazard saved himself by swimming. It is said, that then holding divers books in his hand, he did never let them go, but kept them always upon his head above water, and swam with the other hand, notwithstanding that they shot marvellously at him, and was driven sometime to duck into the water: howbeit the boat was drowned presently. In fine, the king coming to his men that made war with Caesar, he went against him and gave him battle, and won it with great slaughter and effusion of blood. **But [as] for the king, no man could ever tell what became of him after**. Thereupon Caesar made **Cleopatra [the king's] sister, Queen of Egypt**, who being great with child, was shortly brought to bed of a son, whom the Alexandrians named **Caesarion**.

Part Three

From thence he went into Syria, and so going into Asia, there it was told him that [Gnaeus Domitius Calvinus] was overthrown in battle, by Pharnaces, the son of King Mithridates, and was fled out of the realm of Pontus, with a few men with him; and that this King Pharnaces, greedily following his victory, was not contented with the winning of Bithynia, and Cappadocia, but further would needs attempt to win Lesser Armenia, procuring all those kings, princes, and governors of the provinces thereabouts to rebel against the Romans. Thereupon Caesar went thither straight with three legions, and fought a great battle with King Pharnaces, by the city of Zela, where he slew his army, and drove him out of all the realm of Pontus.

And because he would advertise one of his friends of the suddenness of this victory, he only wrote three words unto Anitius at Rome: "Veni, Vidi, Vici": to wit, "I came, I saw, I overcame [*conquered*]." These three words ending all with like sound and letters in the Latin, have a certain short grace, more pleasant to the ear, than can be well expressed in any other tongue.

After this, he returned again into Italy, and came to Rome, ending his year for the which he was made dictator the second time, which office before was never granted for one whole year, but unto him. Then he was chosen consul for the year following [*46 B.C., with Marcus Aemilius Lepidus*].

Narration and Discussion

Caesar's interest in, or obsession with, Cleopatra, has been explored by many artists and storytellers. Do you find the story romantic, or head-shaking?

Fun narration: If you could save a few books from a fire by swimming away with them (like Caesar), which ones would you take?

Lesson Ten

Introduction

Part One covers an important battle in modern-day Tunisia. After Pompey's assassination in Egypt, his allies (the Optimates) had escaped to Roman territory in Africa, and had organized a resistance there. The force was led by Scipio and Marcus Cato the Younger, but involved others such as the two sons of Pompey, and King Juba of Numidia. Caesar and his troops landed in Africa in December of 47 B.C., and the Battle of Thapsus—a siege of the resistance army's stronghold there—took place in February.

In **Part Two**, we have a brief description of the last battle of the civil war: the Battle of Munda against the sons of Pompey.

Shakespeare Connections

Shakespeare's play opens on the day of Caesar's triumph after his victory over the sons of Pompey. "Knew you not Pompey?" demands the tribune Marullus. "And do you now cull out a holiday? / And do you now strew flowers in his way, / That comes in triumph over Pompey's blood?" Shakespeare combines this event with the Feast of Lupercal (in **Lesson Eleven**), at which Caesar is publicly offered, but refuses, a crown. The Lupercal was held in February, but the triumph had actually taken place in October.

Vocabulary

puissant: powerful

predestined: fated, foretold

eftsoons: soon afterward

told him: it's not clear whether Caesar was talking to the eagle or to the ensign bearer

men would never have mistrusted: most would not have attempted

clemency: mercy

the commonwealth: Rome and its provinces and colonies

People

King Juba I (or Iuba): king of Numidia from 60-46 B.C.

Scipio Scallutius: Cornelius Scipio 'Salvito,' a relative of the Roman general Scipio Africanus (see notes for *The Gracchi*)

Afranius: Lucius Afranius, a former consul who supported Pompey

Quintus Fabius Maximus and Quintus Pedius: Caesar's generals in the Battle of Munda

Historic Occasions

46 B.C.: the year with three extra months, because of Caesar's change to the calendar

46 B.C.: the Battle of Thapsus

45 B.C.: the Battle of Munda

Reading

Part One

After the Battle of Pharsalus [**Lessons Eight** and **Nine**], Cato and Scipio being fled into Africa, **King Juba** joined with them, and levied a great **puissant** army. Wherefore Caesar determined to make war with them, and in the midst of winter, he took his journey into Sicily. There, because he would [remove] all hope from his captains and soldiers to make any long abode there, he went and lodged upon the very sands by the seaside, and with the next gale of wind that came, he took the sea with three thousand footmen, and a few horsemen. Then having put them a-land, unawares to them, he hoisted sail again, to go fetch the rest of his army, being afraid least they should meet with some danger in passing over, and meeting them midway, he brought them all into his camp.

Where, when it was told him that his enemies trusted in an ancient oracle, which said that it was **predestined** unto the family of the Scipios to be conquerors in Africa: either of purpose to mock Scipio the general of his enemies, or otherwise in good earnest to take the benefit of this name (given by the oracle) unto himself, in all the skirmishes and battles he fought, [Caesar] gave the charge of his army, unto a man of mean quality and account, called **Scipio Sallutius**, who came of the race of **Scipio Africanus**, and made him always his general when he fought.

For he was **eftsoons** compelled to weary and harry his enemies: for that neither his men in his camp had corn enough, nor his beasts forage, but the soldiers were driven to take seaweeds, called Alga; and (washing away the brackishness thereof with fresh water, putting to it a little herb called dog's tooth), to cast it so to their horse[s] to eat.

For the Numidians (which are light horsemen, and very ready of service) being a great number together, would be on a sudden in every place, and spread all the fields over thereabout, so that no man durst peep out of the camp to go for forage. And one day as the men of arms were staying to behold an African doing notable things in dancing, and playing with the flute: they being set down quietly to take their pleasure of the view thereof, having in the meantime given their slaves their horses to hold, the enemies stealing suddenly upon them, compassed them in round about, and slew a number of them in the field, and, chasing the other[s] also that fled, followed them pell-mell into their camp. Furthermore, had not Caesar himself, and Asinius Pollio with him, gone out of the camp to the rescue, and stayed them that fled: the war that day [would have] been ended.

There was also another skirmish where his enemies had the upper hand, in the which it is reported, that Caesar taking the ensign bearer by the collar that carried the Eagle in his hand, stayed him by force, and turning his face, **told him**: "See, there be thy enemies."

These advantages did lift up Scipio's heart aloft, and gave him courage to hazard battle: and leaving **Afranius** on the one hand of him, and King Juba on the other hand, both their camps lying near to other, he did fortify himself by the city of Thapsus, above the lake, to be a safe refuge for them all in this battle. But whilst he was busy entrenching of himself, Caesar having marvellous speed passed through a great country full of wood, by bypaths which **men would never have mistrusted**: he stole upon some behind, and suddenly assailed the other before, so that he overthrew them all, and made them flee. Then following this first good hap he had, he went forthwith to set upon the camp of Afranius, the which he took at the first onset, and the camp of the Numidians also, King Juba being fled. Thus in a little piece of the day only, he took three camps, and slew fifty thousand of his enemies, and lost but fifty of his soldiers. In this sort is set down the effect of this battle by some writers. Yet others do write also, that Caesar [him]self was not there in person at the execution of this battle. For as he did set his men in battle [ar]ray, the falling sickness took him, whereunto he was given, and therefore feeling it coming, before he was overcome withal, he was carried into a castle not far from thence, where the battle was fought, and there took his rest till the extremity of his disease had left him.

Part Two

After all these things were ended, [Caesar] was chosen consul the fourth time, and went into Spain to make war with the sons of Pompey: who were yet but very young, but had notwithstanding raised a marvellous great army together, and shewed to have had manhood and courage worthy to command such an army, insomuch as they put Caesar himself in great danger of his life.

The greatest battle that was fought between them in all this war, was by the city of Munda. For then Caesar seeing his men sorely distressed, and having their hands full of their enemies: he ran into the press among his men that fought, and cried out unto them: "What, are ye not ashamed to be beaten and taken prisoners, yielding yourselves with your own hands to these young boys?"

And so, with all the force he could make, having with much ado put his enemies to flight: he slew above thirty thousand of them in the field, and lost of his own men a thousand of the best he had. After this battle he went into his tent, and told his friends, that he had often before fought for victory, but this last time now, that he had fought for the safety of his own life. He won this battle on the very feast day of the Bacchanalians, in which men say, that Pompey the Great went out of Rome, about four years before, to begin this civil war. [As for Pompey's sons], the younger escaped from the battle; but within a few days after, Diddius brought the head of the elder. This was the last war that Caesar made.

Julius Caesar

But the triumph he made into Rome for the same, did as much offend the Romans, and more, than anything that ever he had done before: because he had not overcome captains that were strangers, nor barbarous kings, but had destroyed the sons of the noblest man in Rome, whom fortune had overthrown. And because he had plucked up his race by the roots, men did not think it meet for him to triumph so, for the calamities of his country, rejoicing at a thing for the which he had but one excuse to allege in his defence, unto the gods and men: that he was compelled to do that he did. And the rather they thought it not **meet**, because he had never before sent letters nor messengers unto **the commonwealth** at Rome, for any victory that he had ever won in all the civil wars: but did always for shame refuse the glory of it.

This notwithstanding, the Romans inclining to Caesar's prosperity, and taking the bit in the mouth, supposing that to be ruled by one man alone, it would be a good mean[s] for them to take breath a little, after so many troubles and miseries as they had abidden in these civil wars: they chose him perpetual dictator. This was a plain tyranny: for to this absolute power of dictator, they added this: never to be afraid to be deposed. Cicero propounded before the Senate, that they should give him such honours as were meet for a man: howbeit others afterwards added, honours beyond all reason. For, men striving who should most honour him, they made him hateful and troublesome to themselves that most favoured him, by reason of the unmeasurable greatness and honours which they gave him.

Thereupon, it is reported, that even they that most hated him, were no less favourers and furtherers of his honours, than they that most flattered him: because they might have greater occasions to rise, and that it might appear they had just cause and colour to attempt that [which] they did against him. And now for himself, after he had ended his civil wars, he did so honourably behave himself, that there was no fault to be found in him: and therefore methinks, amongst other honours they gave him, he rightly deserved this, that they should build him a temple of **clemency**, to thank him for his courtesy he had used unto them in his victory.

For he pardoned many of them that had borne arms against him, and furthermore, did prefer some of them to honour and office in **the commonwealth**: as amongst others, Cassius and Brutus, both [of] which were made praetors. And where Pompey's images had been thrown down, he caused them to be set up again: whereupon Cicero said then, that [in] Caesar setting up Pompey's images again, he made his own to stand the surer. And when some of his friends did counsel him to have a guard for the safety of his person, and some also did offer themselves to serve him: he would never consent to it, but said, it was better to die once, than always to be afraid of death.

Narration and Discussion

"For, men striving who should most honour him, they made him hateful and troublesome to themselves that most favoured him, by reason of the unmeasurable greatness and honours which they gave him." Is it possible to make someone an enemy by honouring him too much?

Why was Caesar's reaction after the Battle of Munda unusual?

Lesson Eleven

Introduction

Now is a good time to review the things that Julius Caesar did over his long career, to see how things stood at the end of 45 B.C. Who were his friends and his enemies? How did the people of Rome feel about him? Now that the civil wars were over, what did he want or expect? (This could be dramatized as an interview.)

Vocabulary

no place to repair unto: no home

preferments: appointments to high positions

an emulation with himself as with another man: Caesar was almost jealous of himself

magistrates of the commonwealth: rulers of Rome, elders of the people

tearing open his doublet collar: pulling back his toga

proof: test

preferred: proposed, nominated

appointed to be consul: this, obviously, never happened

jealousy: mistrust

pretended: intended

carrion: dead, decaying flesh

People

Brutus, who had in old time driven the kings out of Rome; the first Brutus: the ancestor of this Brutus; see Plutarch's *Life of Publicola*

Historic Occasions

44 B.C.: the conspiracy against Julius Caesar

Shakespeare Connections

"After that, there were set up images of Caesar in the city with diadems upon their heads, like kings. Those, the two tribunes, Flavius and Marullus, went and pulled down: and furthermore, meeting with them that first saluted Caesar as king, they committed them to prison." Shakespeare uses this (and the tribunes) in Act I Scene I, where Flavius says, "Disrobe the images, / If you do find them deck'd with ceremonies...let no images / Be hung with Caesar's trophies." In Scene II, Casca mentions that the tribunes have been "put to silence" for doing so.

In Act I Scene II, Caesar tells Calpurnia to stand directly in Antonius' way when he runs past, and he tells Antonius to make sure he touches Calpurnia. The Lupercal was a fertility festival, and to touch one of the runners might help her bear a son and heir for Caesar.

Antonius says, "When Caesar says, 'Do this,' it is perform'd." When

Caesar reformed the calendar, although it was an improvement to the former system, some people thought it was an additional example of his arrogance. Plutarch quoted Cicero, who once said that if Caesar said, "Tomorow the star Lyra will rise," the response should be "'Yea, at the commandment of Caesar,' as if men were compelled so to say and think, by Caesar's edict."

"Cassius finding Brutus' ambition stirred up the more by these seditious bills, did prick him forward, and egg him on the more, for a private quarrel he had conceived against Caesar." In Act I Scene II, Shakespeare brings this scene to life. In Act II Scene I, Brutus says, "Since Cassius first did whet me against Caesar, / I have not slept."

"As for those fat men and smooth combed heads," quoth he, "I never reckon of them: but these pale-visaged and carrion-lean people, I fear them most," meaning Brutus and Cassius. In Act I Scene II, Shakespeare writes "Let me have men about me that are fat, / Sleek-headed men and such as sleep a-nights. / Yond Cassius has a lean and hungry look, / He thinks too much; such men are dangerous."

During the Lupercal, Brutus hears shouting but doesn't see what happened. Afterwards he asks **Casca** for his narration of the events. "I saw Mark Antony offer him a crown—yet 'twas not a crown neither, 'twas one of these coronets..." Shakespeare adds a bit more drama to the scene by saying that Caesar then "fell down in the market-place, and foam'd at mouth, and was speechless"; and that (according to Casca) "he pluck'd me ope his doublet; and offer'd them his throat to cut." This is something that Plutarch describes just before the scene at the Lupercal, in **Part Two**.

Reading

Part One

But to win himself the love and good will of the people, as the honourablest guard and best safety he could have: [Julius Caesar] made common feasts again, and general distributions of corn. Furthermore, to gratify the soldiers also, he replenished many cities again with inhabitants, which before had been destroyed, and placed them there that had **no place to repair unto**: of the which the noblest and chiefest cities were these two, Carthage, and Corinth, and it chanced so, that like as aforetime they had been both taken and destroyed together, even so were they both set afoot again, and replenished with people, at one self time.

And as for great personages, he won them also, promising some of them, to make them praetors and consuls in time to come, and unto others, honours and **preferments**, but to all men generally good hope, seeking all the ways he could to make every man contented with his reign. The prosperous good success he had of his former conquests bred no desire in him quietly to enjoy the fruits of his labours, but rather gave him hope of things to come, still kindling more and more in him thoughts of greater enterprises, and desire of new glory, as if that which he had present, were stale and nothing worth. This humour of his was no other but **an emulation with himself as with another man**, and a certain contention to overcome the things he prepared to attempt. For he was determined, and made preparation also, to make war with the Persians...and so to enlarge the Roman Empire round, that it might be every way compassed in with the Great Sea Oceanum.

[Caesar had many other plans and ideas, some of which were carried out and some not. One idea that he did put into action was the reworking of the calendar.]

Part Two

But the chiefest cause that made him mortally hated, was the covetous desire he had to be called king: which first gave the people just cause, and next his secret enemies, honest colour to bear him ill will. This notwithstanding, they that procured him this honour and dignity, gave it out among the people that it was written in the prophecies, how the Romans might overcome the Parthians, if they made war with them, and were led by a king, but otherwise that they were unconquerable. And furthermore, they were so bold besides, that Caesar returning to Rome from the city of Alba, when they came to salute him, they called him king. But the people being offended, and Caesar also angry, he said he was not called king, but Caesar. Then every man keeping silence, he went his way heavy and sorrowful.

When they had decreed divers honours for him in the Senate, the consuls and praetors, accompanied with the whole assembly of the Senate, went unto him in the marketplace, where he was set by the pulpit for orations, to tell him what honours they had decreed for him in his absence. But he sitting still in his majesty, disdaining to rise up unto them when they came in, as if they had been private men, answered them: that his honours had more need to be cut off, than enlarged. This did not only offend the Senate, but the common people also, to see that he should so lightly esteem of the **magistrates of the commonwealth**: insomuch as every man that might lawfully go his way, departed thence very sorrowfully. Thereupon also Caesar rising, departed home to his house, and **tearing open his doublet collar**, making his neck bare, he cried out aloud to his friends that his throat was ready to offer to any man that would come and cut it. Notwithstanding, it is reported, that afterwards to excuse this folly, he imputed it to his disease, saying, that their wits are not perfect which have his disease of the falling evil, when standing of their feet they speak to the common people, but are soon troubled with a trembling of their body, and a sudden dimness and giddiness.

But that was not true. For he would have risen up to the Senate, but Cornelius Balbus one of his friends (but rather a flatterer) would not let him, saying: "What, do you not remember that you are Caesar, and will you not let them reverence you, and do their duties?"

Part Three

[*The Feast of Lupercal was a Roman religious festival that included a foot race through the streets.*]

Caesar sat to behold that sport upon the pulpit for orations, in a chair of gold, apparelled in triumphing manner. Antonius, who was consul at that time, was one of them that ran this holy course. So when he came into the marketplace, the people made a lane for him to run at liberty, and he came to Caesar, and presented him a diadem wreathed about with laurel. Whereupon there rose a certain cry of rejoicing, not very great, done only by a few, appointed for the purpose. But when Caesar refused the diadem, then all the people together made an outcry of joy. Then Antonius offering it him again, there was a second shout of joy, but yet of a few. But when Caesar refused it again the second time, then all the whole people shouted. Caesar having made this **proof**, found that the people did not like of it, and thereupon rose out of his chair, and commanded the crown to be carried unto Jupiter in the Capitol.

After that, there were set up images of Caesar in the city with diadems upon their heads, like kings. Those, the two tribunes, Flavius and Marullus, went and pulled down; and furthermore, meeting with them that first saluted Caesar as king, they committed them to prison. The people followed them rejoicing at it, and called them *Brutes*: because of **Brutus, who had in old time driven the kings out of Rome**, and that brought the kingdom of one person, unto the government of the Senate and people. Caesar was so offended withal, that he deprived Marullus and Flavius of their tribuneships, and accusing them, he spake also against the people, and called them *Bruti* and *Cumani*, to wit, beasts and fools. Hereupon the people went straight unto Marcus Brutus, who from his father came of **the first Brutus**, and by his mother, of the house of the Servilians, a noble house as any was in Rome, and was also nephew and son in law of [the late] Marcus Cato (the Younger). Notwithstanding, the great honours and favour Caesar shewed unto him, kept him back that of himself alone, he did not conspire nor consent to depose him of his kingdom.

For Caesar did not only save his life, after the Battle of Pharsalus when Pompey fled, and did at his request also save many more of his friends besides: but furthermore, he put a marvellous confidence in him. For he had already **preferred** him to the praetorship for that year; and furthermore was **appointed to be consul**, the fourth year after that, having through Caesar's friendship obtained it before Cassius, who likewise made suit for the same: and Caesar also, as it is reported, said in this contention: "Indeed Cassius hath alleged best reason, but yet shall he not be chosen before Brutus." Some [people] one day accusing Brutus [of practising] this conspiracy, Caesar would not hear of it, but clapping his hand on his body, told them, 'Brutus will look for this skin": meaning thereby, that Brutus for his virtue, deserved to rule after him, but yet, that for ambition's sake, he would not shew himself unthankful nor dishonourable. Now they that desired change, and wished Brutus only their prince and governor above all other:[s] they durst not come to him themselves to tell him what they would have him to do, but in the night did cast sundry papers into the praetor's seat where he gave audience, most of them to this effect: "Thou sleepest Brutus, and art not Brutus indeed." Cassius finding Brutus' ambition stirred up the more by these seditious bills, did prick him forward, and egg him on the more, for a private quarrel he had conceived against Caesar: the circumstance whereof, we have set down more at large in Brutus' *Life*.

Caesar also had Cassius in great **jealousy**, and suspected him much: whereupon he said on a time to his friends, "What will Cassius do, think ye? I like not his pale looks. " Another time when Caesar's friends complained unto him of Antonius, and Dolabella, that they **pretended** some mischief towards him: he answered them again, "As for those fat men and smooth-combed heads," quoth he, "I never reckon of them: but these pale-visaged and **carrion**-lean people, I fear them most," meaning Brutus and Cassius.

Narration and Discussion

Did Caesar want to be a king? Was he already a king in everything but name?

Why did Caesar say that he distrusted pale, thin people?

Lesson Twelve

Introduction

As you read the assassination scene, watch for differences between what you may have seen or read in other sources, and what Plutarch actually said (for instance, about Caesar's last words).

Not you too?

Shakespeare's Julius Caesar says "Et tu, Brute?" to Brutus, and those words are quoted today as an accusation to a traitorous friend. The historian Suetonius said that the remark was something like "You too, son?" But Plutarch said that when Caesar died, he had pulled his toga over his head, so nobody knows what his last words were.

Shakespeare Connections

In Act I Scene I, we have the famous scene with the soothsayer: "Beware the Ides of March!"

Act I Scene III begins on the evening before the murder, with **Casca**, breathless and fearful, describing some of the things he has seen. "Whoever knew the heavens menace so?" **Cassius** says to Casca that these natural or supernatural phenomena are all symbols of Caesar, "a man / Most like this dreadful night."

Acts II and III continue the story, and there are many points of comparison with Plutarch's text. Act IV begins with the dealings between Mark Antony, Octavius, and Lepidus; and then moves on to focus on Cassius and Brutus. The ghostly messenger ("the ghost of Caesar") appears to Brutus in Act IV, Scene III.

Cassius dies in Act V Scene III, and Brutus in Scene V. Shakespeare added his own dramatic ending, with Antonius and Octavius making speeches over the body of Brutus.

Vocabulary

mortal: fatal, deadly

as though he would have said...: as if he wanted to say something about what had happened

Caesar's testament: his will

forms: benches

firebrands: torches

an ague: a fever

counsellors: those who planned the murder

dispatched him: killed him

People

Publius Servilius *Casca* Longus (84 BC – c. 42 BC): one of the assassins of Gaius Julius Caesar; see introductory notes

Metellus Cimber: the client that Caesar was representing, but who was also part of the conspiracy

Octavius Caesar the younger: later called Caesar Augustus

Historic Occasions

March 15, 44 B.C.: The Ides of March (the death of Julius Caesar)

October, 42 B.C.: the deaths of Gaius Cassius Longinus and Marcius Junius Brutus

Reading

Part One

Certainly, destiny may easier be foreseen than avoided: considering the strange and wonderful signs that were said to be seen before Caesar's death.

[Omitted for length: specific omens and happenings.]

Furthermore, there was a certain soothsayer that had given Caesar warning long time afore, to take heed of the day of the Ides of March (which is the fifteenth of the month), for on that day he should be in great danger. That day being come, Caesar going unto the Senate house, and speaking merrily to the soothsayer, told him. "The Ides of March be come." "So be they," softly answered the soothsayer, "but yet are they not past." And the very day before, Caesar supping with Marcus Lepidus, sealed certain letters as he was wont to do at the board: so talk falling out amongst them, reasoning what death was best: he preventing their opinions, cried out aloud, "Death unlooked for."

Then going to bed the same night as his manner was, and lying with his wife Calpumia, all the windows and doors of his chamber flying open, the noise awoke him, and made him afraid when he saw such light: but more, when he heard his wife Calpurnia, being fast asleep, weep and sigh, and put forth many fumbling lamentable speeches. For she dreamed that Caesar was slain, and that she had him in her arms. Others also do deny that she had any such dream, as amongst other[s], Titus Livius writeth, that it was in this sort. The Senate having set upon the top of Caesar's house, for an ornament and setting forth of the same, a certain pinnacle: Calpurnia dreamed that she saw it broken down, and that she thought she lamented and wept for it.

Insomuch that Caesar rising in the morning, she prayed him if it were possible, not to go out of the doors that day, but to adjourn the session of the Senate until another day. And if that he made no reckoning of her dream, yet that he would search further of the soothsayers by their sacrifices, to know what should happen him that day. Thereby it seemed that Caesar likewise did fear and suspect somewhat, because his wife Calpurnia until that time, was never given to any fear or superstition: and then, for that he saw her so troubled in mind with this dream she had. But much more afterwards, when the soothsayers having sacrificed many beasts one after another, told him that none did like them: then he determined to send Antonius to adjourn the session of the Senate.

[Decius Brutus Albinus, who was part of the conspiracy, came to Caesar's house and convinced him not to listen to the soothsayers, and that he needed to attend the Senate meeting. This might be an interesting place to incorporate the scene from Shakespeare's play.]

So Caesar coming into the house, all the Senate stood up on their feet to do him honour. Then part of Brutus' company and confederates stood round about Caesar's chair, and part of them also came towards him, as though they made suit with **Metellus Cimber**, to call home his brother again from banishment: and thus prosecuting still their suit, they followed Caesar, till he was set in his chair. Who, denying their petitions, and being offended with them one after another, because the more they were denied, the more they pressed upon him, and were the earnester with him: **Metellus** at length, taking his gown with both his hands, pulled it over his neck, which was the sign given the confederates to set upon him.

Then Casca behind him strake him in the neck with his sword, howbeit the wound was not great nor **mortal**, because it seemed, the fear of such a devilish attempt did amaze him, and take his strength from him, that he killed him not at the first blow. But Caesar turning straight unto him, caught hold of his sword, and held it hard: and they both cried out, Caesar in Latin: "O vile traitor Casca, what doest thou?" and Casca in Greek to his brother, "Brother, help me."

At the beginning of this stir, they that were present, not knowing of the conspiracy, were so amazed with the horrible sight they saw: that they had no power to flee, neither to help him, not so much as once to make any outcry. They on the other side that had conspired his death, compassed him in on every side with their swords drawn in their hands, that Caesar turned him nowhere, but he was stricken at by some, and still had naked swords in his face, and was hacked and mangled among them, as a wild beast taken of hunters. For it was agreed among them, that every man should give him a wound, because all their parts should be in this murder. Men report also, that Caesar did still defend himself against the rest, running every way with his body: but when he saw Brutus with his sword drawn in his hand, then he pulled his gown over his head, and made no more resistance.

Part Two

When Caesar was slain, the [senators] (though Brutus stood in the midst amongst them **as though he would have said somewhat touching this fact**) presently ran out of the house, and fleeing, filled all the city with marvellous fear and tumult. Insomuch as some did shut their doors, others forsook their shops and warehouses, and others ran to the place to see what the matter was: and others also that had seen it, ran home to their houses again. But Antonius and Lepidus, which were two of Caesar's chiefest friends, secretly conveying themselves away, fled into other men's houses, and forsook their own.

Brutus and his confederates on the other side, being yet hot with this murder they had committed, having their swords drawn in their hands, came all in a troop together out of the Senate, and went into the marketplace, not as men that made countenance to flee, but otherwise boldly holding up their heads like men of courage, and called to the people to defend their liberty, and stayed to speak with every great personage whom they met in their way. Of them, some followed this troop, and went amongst them, as if they had been of the conspiracy, and falsely challenged part of the honour with them: among them [were] Gaius Octavius and Lentulus Spinther. But both of them were afterwards put to death, for their vain covetousness of honour, by Antonius and **Octavius Caesar the younger**: and yet had no part of that honour for the which they were put to death, neither did any man believe that they were any of the confederates, or of counsel with them. For they that did put them to death, took revenge rather of the will they had to offend, than of any fact they had committed.

Part Three

The next morning, Brutus and his confederates came into the marketplace to speak unto the people, who gave them such audience, that it seemed they neither greatly reproved, nor allowed the fact: for by their great silence they showed, that they were sorry for Caesar's death, and also that they did reverence Brutus. Now the Senate granted general pardon for all that was past, and to pacify every man, ordained besides, that Caesar's funerals should be honoured as a god, and established all things that he had done: and gave certain provinces also, and convenient honours unto Brutus and his confederates, whereby every man thought all things were brought to good peace and quietness again.

But when they had opened **Caesar's testament**, and found a liberal legacy of money, bequeathed unto every citizen of Rome, and that they saw his body (which was brought into the marketplace) all bemangled with gashes of swords: then there was no order to keep the multitude and common people quiet, but they plucked up **forms**, tables, and stools, and laid them all about the body, and setting them a fire, burnt the corpse. Then when the fire was well kindled, they took the **firebrands**, and went unto their houses that had slain Caesar, to set them afire. Other also ran up and down the city to see if they could meet with any of them, to cut them in pieces: howbeit they could meet with never a man of them, because they had locked themselves up safely in their houses.

There was one of Caesar's friends called Cinna, that had a

marvellous strange and terrible dream the night before. He dreamed that Caesar bade him to supper, and that he refused, and would not go: then that Caesar took him by the hand, and led him against his will. Now Cinna hearing at that time, that they burnt Caesar's body in the marketplace, notwithstanding that he feared his dream, and had **an ague** on him besides: he went into the marketplace to honour his funerals. When he came thither, one of mean sort asked what his name was? He was straight called by his name. The first man told it to another, and that other unto another, so that it ran straight through them all, that he was one of them that murdered Caesar: (for indeed one of the traitors to Caesar, was also called Cinna as himself) wherefore taking him for Cinna the murderer, they fell upon him with such fury, that they presently dispatched him in the marketplace.

This stir and fury made Brutus and Cassius more afraid, than of all that was past, and therefore within [a] few days after, they departed out of Rome: and touching their doings afterwards, and what calamity they suffered till their deaths, we have written it at large, in the *Life of Brutus*.

Caesar died at six and fifty years of age: and Pompey also lived not passing four years more than he. So he reaped no other fruit of all his reign and dominion, which he had so vehemently desired all his life, and pursued with such extreme danger: but a vain name only, and a superficial glory, that procured him the envy and hatred of his country. But his great prosperity and good fortune that favoured him all his lifetime, did continue afterwards in the revenge of his death, pursuing the murderers both by sea and land, till they had not left a man more to be executed, of all them that were actors or **counsellors** in the conspiracy of his death.

Part Four (Epilogue)

Furthermore, of all the chances that happen unto men upon the earth, that which came to Cassius above all other[s], is most to be wondered at. For he, being overcome in battle at the journey of Philippi, slew himself with the same sword with which he strake Caesar.

Again, of signs in the element, the great comet which seven nights together was seen very bright after Caesar's death, the eight[th] night after was never seen more. Also the brightness of the sun was darkened, the which all that year through rose very pale, and shined not out, whereby it gave but small heat: therefore the air being very cloudy and dark, by the weakness of the heat that could not come forth, did cause the earth to bring forth but raw and unripe fruit, which rotted before it could ripe[n].

But above all, the ghost that appeared unto Brutus shewed plainly, that the gods were offended with the murder of Caesar. The vision was thus: Brutus being ready to pass over his army from the city of Abydos, to the other coast lying directly against it, slept every night (as his manner was) in his tent, and being yet awake, thinking of his affairs: (for by report he was as careful a captain, and lived with as little sleep, as ever man did) he thought he heard a noise at his tent door, and looking towards the light of the lamp that waxed very dim, he saw a horrible vision of a man, of a wonderful greatness, and dreadful look, which at the first made him marvellously afraid. But when he saw that it did him no hurt, but stood by his bedside, and said nothing: at length he asked him what he was. The image answered him: "I am thy ill angel, Brutus, and thou shalt see me by the city of Philippi." Then Brutus replied again, and said: "Well, I shall see thee then." Therewithal, the spirit presently vanished from him.

After that time Brutus being in battle near unto the city of Philippi, against Antonius and Octavius Caesar, at the first battle he won the victory, and overthrowing all them that withstood him, he drave them into young Caesar's camp, which he took. The second battle being at hand, this spirit appeared again unto him, but spake never a word. Thereupon Brutus knowing he should die, did put himself to all hazard in battle, but yet fighting could not be slain. So seeing his men put to flight and overthrown, he ran unto a little rock not far off, and there setting his sword's point to his breast, fell upon it, and slew himself, but yet as it is reported, with the help of his friend, that **dispatched him**.

Narration and Discussion

The story of the life of Julius Caesar ends with Plutarch's pronouncement that "he reaped no other fruit of all his reign and dominion, which he had so vehemently desired all his life, and pursued with such extreme danger: but a vain name only, and a superficial glory, that procured him the envy and hatred of his country." Did Caesar end up with a vain name only?

Shakespeare turned his attention, at the end of the play, to Brutus, calling him "the noblest Roman of them all." This may be partly because he used Plutarch's *Life of Brutus* as extra source material for the play, and also to create a contrast with Caesar. In this *Life*, we have not heard much about Brutus, other than the fact that Caesar pardoned him for his support of Pompey. Is it surprising that Plutarch ended the story in this way?

Agis and Cleomenes

(Third Century B.C.)

Introduction

"When the people heard what he said, they marvelled much at the noble mind of this young king, and were very glad of it, saying: that for three hundred years' space together, the city of Sparta had not so worthy a king as he."

Popular images of cultures, peoples, and places do not always recognize the effects of time and world events on those cultures. School lessons on "Ancient Egypt," for example, might focus on the age of Tutankhamun, in about 1300 B.C., but miss the point that the Great Pyramid was built over a thousand years before that. Ancient history, so to speak, to King Tut. "Ancient Rome" includes at least a thousand years of change. A study of North American or British culture over the past five hundred years would be meaningless without an understanding of the events, discoveries, and shifts in government that influenced daily life. Students in future centuries might imagine a Victorian-era man, wearing a suit of armour, texting his friends about enlisting in George Washington's army.

When we study the Spartans, we often have an image of their militaristic culture at its peak, around 600-400 B.C. Even Plutarch, writing about that early age, describes them as a people raised in a kind of boot camp, whose ideal was to die gloriously in battle. The heroic deaths at Thermopylae took place in 480 B.C. By 404 B.C., Sparta had defeated Athens in the Second Peloponnesian War..

But Sparta's season of power was ending, and within a few years it was unexpectedly beaten in the landmark Battle of Leuctra with the Thebans. By the time the story of Agis and Cleomenes began, just over a hundred years later in 245 B.C., Sparta had become a different place. Ancient laws and traditions attributed to the (possibly mythical) lawgiver Lycurgus had been shoved aside. The rule that property must be inherited by family members, rather than bought or sold at will, was now irrelevant; the rich were getting richer by scooping up land. The majority of people living in the city were not Spartan citizens, so they had no particular interest in maintaining the old ideals of military discipline, or even in defending their state if it was threatened.

If the Spartans could have looked ahead another hundred years, they would have been even more shocked to know that all of Greece would then be conquered by Rome. However, in the reigns of Agis and Cleomenes, Sparta thought it still might be able to recover its old identity and power. The problem was how to go about it.

Names, Places, and Words to Know

What is Lacedaemon? What is Laconia? What is Laconic?

For our purposes, Sparta/Spartan and Lacedaemon/Lacedaemonian are synonymous. Laconia is the region in which Sparta/Lacedaemon was located, although Lacedaemon (or Lacedaemonia) is used also to refer to the region rather than the city.

Laconic can mean anything in or of Laconia, but it also refers to Spartan traditions in clothing, diet, etc. A "Laconic answer" is brief, with no words wasted.

What is the Peloponnesus? What is Achaea? Who was Aratus?

The Peloponnesus is the southern part of Greece, the part connected to the north by the Isthmus of Corinth. Achaea was the name of a group of states in the Peloponnesus, and the **Achaean League** was a confederacy of these states, led at that time by General Aratus of Sicyon.

What are the Argives? Who was Aristomachus?

The Argives were the inhabitants of the city of Argos, a one-time rival of Sparta. Aristomachus was the ruler of Argos.

What is Messena? Megalopolis?

Messena or Messene (in the region of Messenia) and Megalopolis (in Arcadia) were two fortified cities in the Peloponnesus. They were built in an attempt to protect their citizens from further rule by outsiders (that is, by the Spartans).

What is the Race of Hercules?

Sparta was ruled by two hereditary kings, one each from the Eurypontid and the Agiad dynasties (both of whom were supposed to be descended from Heracles/Hercules). The kings were assisted by the **Gerousia**, a council of elders ("old men") who were elected for life. There were also five elected officials called **ephors**.

This *Life* is unusual because it includes the stories of two kings. (Dryden's translation separates the two.) The first few lessons are about Agis IV, the 25th king of the Eurypontid dynasty (see the chart below), and his co-ruler, Leonidas II, the 28th king of the Agiad dynasty. The second part is the story of the son and successor of Leonidas, Cleomenes III.

Two Spartan Dynasties

Eurypontids

Agis IV: succeeded his father as king in 245 B.C., and reigned four years before his death in 241 B.C.

Eudamidas III: son of Agis IV, a child king who "reigned" from 241 to 228 B.C. but who never really had power

Archidamus V: the brother of Agis IV; reigned from 228–227 B.C. (when he was assassinated)

Eucleidas or Euclidas: an Agiad by heredity, but he ruled with his brother Cleomenes until he was killed at the Battle of Selasia in 222 B.C.

Lycurgus: not the ancient lawgiver but a later Spartan king (219 B.C.)

Agiads

Leonidas II: reigned 254 to 235 B.C. Temporarily replaced by his son-in-law **Cleombrotus II** from 242-241 B.C., who was afterwards sent into exile.

Cleomenes III: the son of Leonidas II, who succeeded him and reigned from 235–222 B.C. He seems to have been a bit younger than Agis, because in 241 B.C. he was considered slightly too young to marry.

Agesipolis III: the last of the Agiad kings, the grandson of Cleombrotus II. After the death of Cleomenes III, he became king while still a boy, but was soon deposed by Lycurgus (see above).

Who was Antigonus?

Antigonus III Doson was the king of Macedon. He was around the same age as Agis and Cleomenes, and ruled from 229 B.C. until his death in 221 B.C. The study guide for Plutarch's *Life of Philopoemen* includes this note: "The year was 222 B.C., and Philopoemen was about 30 years old. He joined with the Macedonians (King Antigonus III, also called Antigonus Doson) to oust the king of Sparta (Cleomenes III) from Megalopolis. Although Antigonus was a bit annoyed that Philopoemen took control and led a charge without being ordered to, he had to admit that Philopoemen 'did like an experienced commander' (Dryden's translation)."

Who was Ptolemy? Which one?

Ptolemy III Euergetes was the third ruler of the Ptolemaic dynasty of Egypt; the "old" King Ptolemy, who died soon after Cleomenes' arrival in 222 B.C. **Ptolemy IV Philopator** was the king who mistrusted Cleomenes (and was responsible for the deaths of his own mother Berenice and brother Magas). There are also two other men named **Ptolemy** mentioned in **Lesson Twelve**.

Names That Are Easy to Confuse

Agis, **Agesilaus** (his uncle), **Archidamus** (his brother), **Agesistrata** (his mother), **Archidamia** (his grandmother), and **Agiatis** (his wife, later married to Cleomenes). *(To make it more confusing, Agis and his family were not Agiads, but Eurypontids.)* Also **Aratus, Antigonus, Agesipolis**, and **Aristomachus.**

Cleombrotus (see above) vs. **Cleomenes** (see above)

Cratesiclea (mother of Cleomenes) vs. **Agesistrata** (mother of Agis)

Lycurgus vs. **Leonidas** vs. **Lysander** vs. **Lysiadas** (Lydiadas)

Lesson One

Introduction

In 245 B.C., the Greek city-state of Sparta had fallen into corruption. The Spartans had forgotten the laws set down for them by Lycurgus, including their style of dress and rules of inheritance. Traditionally, Spartan citizens could leave property only to their relatives, and this seemed to keep the economy stable and most people satisfied. Now properties were being bought and sold freely, causing some people to become very rich and others to fall into poverty. Could King Agis convince everyone, including his co-ruler King Leonidas, to go back to the old system?

Vocabulary

voluptuousness and licentious life: unrestrained, self-indulgent behaviour

a battle fought before the city of Plataea: the Battle of Plataea, during the Persian War

never liked the people: never suited the people

the commonwealth: the Spartan state and its dependencies

Leonidas of all other exceeded: he was the worst of them all

magnanimity: greatness of soul or spirit

by succession from their fathers: by inheritance

Lycurgus' first ordinance and institution: the original Spartan laws

did yet preserve the commonwealth...: kept things from falling into an even worse state

seditious: rebellious

preferred: proposed

by testament: by writing a will

honest sciences: honourable pursuits

natural citizens of Sparta: members of the old Spartan families

no countenance nor calling: no wealth or honour (Dryden)

strait: narrow, strict

runagate: renegade, rebel

pricked forward: motivated, encouraged

changing of the state and commonwealth: a change in government

making her privy unto it: telling her about it

depart with her goods: give up her money or property

slaves and factors: Dryden translates this "followers and menials"

People

Lysander, Mandroclidas, Agesilaus: men of power in Sparta

Historic Occasions

245 B.C.: Agis became king of Sparta

Reading

[When the] covetousness of gold and silver crept again into the city of Sparta, and with riches, covetousness also and misery, and by use, **voluptuousness and licentious life**: Sparta was then void of all honour and goodness, and was long time drowned in shame and dishonour, until King[s] Agis and Leonidas came to reign there.

Agis was of the house of the Eurypontides, the son of Eudamidas, the sixth of lineal descent after Agesilaus, who had been the greatest prince of all Greece in his time. Leonidas also, the son of Cleonymus, was of the other family of the Agiades, the eight[h] of succession after Pausanias, who slew Mardonius, the King's Lieutenant General of Persia, in **a battle fought before the city of Plataea.** Howbeit his manners and conditions **never liked the people.** For though all men generally were corrupted through **the commonwealth,** and clean out of order: yet **Leonidas of all other exceeded,** deforming most the ancient Laconian life, because he had been long time brought up in princes' houses [*in Persia*], and followed also Seleucus' court, from whence he had brought all the pride and pomp of those courts into Greece, where law and reason ruleth.

Agis, on the contrary part, did not only far excel Leonidas, in honour and **magnanimity** of mind: but all other[s] almost also which had reigned in Sparta, from the time of Agesilaus the Great. So that when Agis was not yet twenty years old, and being daintily brought up with the fineness of two women, his mother Agesistrata, and Archidamia his grandmother, which had more gold and silver, than all the Lacedaemonians else: he began to spurn against these womanish delights and pleasures, [such as] in making himself fair to be the better beliked, and to be fine and trim in his apparel; and [instead] to cast upon him a plain Spartan cape, taking pleasure in the diet, baths, and manner of the ancient Laconian life: and [he] openly boasted besides, that he would not desire to be king, but only for the hope he had to restore the ancient Laconian life by his authority.

[*A flashback*]

The state of Lacedaemon first [began] to be corrupted, and to leave her ancient discipline, when the Lacedaemonians having subdued the empire of the Athenians, stored themselves and country both, with plenty of gold and silver. But yet reserving still the lands left unto them **by succession from their fathers**, according unto **Lycurgus' first ordinance and institution**, for division of the lands amongst them: which **ordinance**, and equality being inviolably kept amongst them, **did yet preserve the commonwealth from defamation of divers other notorious crimes**. [This lasted] until the time of the authority of Epitadeus, one of the ephors, a **seditious** man, and of proud conditions: who bitterly falling out with his own son, **preferred** a law, that every man might lawfully give his lands and goods whilst he lived, or after his death **by testament,** unto any man whom he liked or thought well of. Thus this man made this law to satisfy his anger, and others also did confirm it for covetousness' sake, and so overthrew a noble ordinance. For the rich men then began to buy lands of numbers, and so transferred it from the right and lawful heirs: whereby a few men in short time being made very rich, immediately after there fell out great poverty in the city of Sparta, which made all **honest sciences** to cease, and brought in thereupon unlawful occupations, [and the poor] envied them that were wealthy. Therefore, there remained not above seven hundred **natural citizens of Sparta** in all, and of them, not above a hundred that had lands and inheritance: for all the rest were poor people in the city, and were of **no countenance nor calling**. Besides that, they went unwillingly to the wars against their enemies, looking every day for stir and change in the city.

[*Back to the story*]

Agis therefore thinking it a notable good act (as indeed it was) to replenish the city of Sparta again, and to bring in the old equality, he moved the matter unto the citizens. He found the youth (against all hope) to give good ear unto him, and very well given unto virtue, easily changing their garments and life, to recover their liberty again. But the oldest men, which were now even rotten with covetousness and corruption, they were afraid to return again to the **strait** ordinances of Lycurgus, as a slave and **runagate** from his master, that trembleth when he is brought back again unto him. Therefore they reproved Agis, when he did lament before them their present miserable estate, and wish also for the former ancient honour and true dignity of Sparta.

Howbeit **Lysander** the son of Libys, and **Mandroclidas** the son of Ecphanes, and **Agesilaus** also, greatly commended his noble desire, and persuaded him to go forward withal. **Agesilaus**, the king's uncle, and an eloquent man, was very effeminate and covetous, and yet **pricked forward** to give his furtherance to this attempt, as it appeared, by his son Hippomedon, who was a notable good soldier, and could do very much by means of the love and good-will the young men did bear him. But indeed, the secret cause that brought Agesilaus to consent unto [the proposals of Agis], was the greatness of his debt which he owed, of the which he hoped to be discharged by **changing of the state and commonwealth**.

Now when Agis had won him [Agesilaus], he [Agis] sought by his means to draw his mother also unto the matter, which was Agesilaus' sister. She could do very much by the number of her friends, followers, and debtors in the city, by whose means she ruled the most part of the affairs of the city after her own pleasure. But the young man Hippomedon **making her privy unto it**, at the first she was amazed withal, and bade him hold his peace if he were wise, and not meddle in matters unpossible and unprofitable. But when Agesilaus had told her what a notable act it would be, and how easily it might be brought to pass, with marvellous great profit: and that King Agis began also to strain her with great entreaty, that she should willingly **depart with her goods** to win her son honour and glory: who, though he could not in money and riches come to be like unto other kings (because the **slaves and factors** [alone] of Kings Seleucus and Ptolemy had more money than all the kings of Sparta had together that ever reigned). Yet if in temperance, thriftiness, and noble mind (exceeding all their vanities) he could come to restore the Lacedaemonians again unto equality [with each other], then indeed he should be counted a noble king.

Narration and Discussion

How did the issue of property ownership create such a bad effect on the rest of Spartan life, such as causing "all honest sciences to cease?" (Is it wrong for people to buy land?)

Why did Agis believe that getting his people back "under the law" would actually be liberating for them? (Read Psalm 119:1-12.)

For older students or those who want to go deeper: Compare the strict Spartan laws laid out by Lycurgus to those of the Israelites, especially regarding property inheritance, the Year of Jubilee, clothing, diet, and marriage to foreigners.

Lesson Two

Introduction

Agis used his new power as king to propose a one-time cancellation of debts, and re-distribution of land among both the old families and newcomers who were willing to fight for Sparta. To show his seriousness, Agis was the first to put his his own land up for division. However, the elders and ephors (particularly those who had a lot of land or who were owed money) wanted to take things more slowly.

Vocabulary

suffering: allowing

felicity: happiness; in this case, delight and joy

let that this enterprise...: prevent this from happening

tyranny: rule (not necessarily tyranny as we understand it)

preferred, preferring: proposed, proposing

the commonwealth: the state

the Senate: the Council of Elders or **Gerousia** (see introductory note)

this commonwealth: the Spartan state

all his arable and pasture he had: his inherited land or patrimony

ready money: cash (vs. something promised for later)

indifferently: without exception

make their goods in common: share what they had

strange: foreign

the success hereof: this happening

Juno, surnamed Chalceaecos: Dryden translates this "Minerva of the Brazen House"; the temple is also called "Athena Chalcioecus"

making default, they deposed him: he did not appear in court, so they de-throned him

against the law: they had enacted the reform without the majority of elders agreeing to it

jar: disagreement

vice: evil

[e]stablish both together: enact both the land reform and the abolishing of debts

usurers: money-lenders who charge unfairly high interest rates

Reading

Part One

These women being stirred up with ambition by these persuasions of the young man, seeing him so nobly bent, as if by the gods their minds had secretly been inflamed with the love of virtue: did presently alter their minds in such sort, that they themselves did prick forward Agis, and sent for their friends to pray and entreat them to favour his enterprise: and furthermore, they brought on other women also, knowing that the Lacedaemonians did ever hear and believe their wives, **suffering** them to understand more of the affairs of the state, than they [the men] themselves did of their private estate at home.

Herein is to be considered, that the most part of the riches of Lacedaemon was in the hands of the women, and therefore they were against it, not only because thereby they were cut off from their fineness and excess, in the which being ignorant of the true good indeed, they put all their **felicity**: but also, because they saw their honour and authority which they had by their riches, clean trodden underfoot. Therefore they coming to Leonidas, they did persuade him to reprove Agis, because he was [an] elder man than he, and to **let that this enterprise went not forward**. Leonidas did what he could in favour of the rich, but fearing the common people, who desired nothing but alteration, he durst not openly speak against him, but secretly he did the best he could to hinder Agis' practice, talking with the magistrates of the city: and accusing Agis unto them, he told them how he did offer the rich men's goods unto the poor, the division of their lands, and the abolishing of all debts, [with the real aim] to put the **tyranny** into his hands, and that thereby he got him a strong guard unto himself, but not many citizens unto Sparta.

This notwithstanding, King Agis having procured Lysander to be chosen one of the ephors, he presently **preferred** his law unto the council. The articles whereof were these:

> That such as were in debt, should be cleared of all
> their debts, and that the lands also should be
> divided into equal parts: so that from the Valley of
> Pallena unto Mount Taugetus, and unto the cities of
> Malea, and Selasia, there should be four thousand
> five hundred parts, and without those bounds, there
> should be in all the rest, fifteen thousand parts, the
> which should be distributed unto their neighbours
> meet to carry weapon: and the rest unto the natural
> Spartans. The number of them should be
> replenished with their neighbours and strangers in
> like manner, which should be very well brought up,
> and be able men besides to serve **the
> commonwealth**: all the which afterwards should
> be divided into fifteen companies, of the which,
> some should receive two hundred, and others four

hundred men, and should live according to the old
ancient institution observed by their ancestors.

This law being **preferred** unto **the Senate**, the senators grew to
divers opinions upon it. Whereupon Lysander himself assembled the
great council of all the people, and there spake unto them himself,
and Mandroclidas, and Agesilaus also, praying them not to suffer the
honour of Sparta to be trodden underfoot, for the vanity of a few.

When every man else had spoken, King Agis rising up, briefly
speaking unto the people, said that he would bestow great
contributions for the reformation of **this commonwealth**, which he
was desirous to restore again. For first of all, he would make
common **all his arable and pasture he had**, and besides that, he
would add six hundred talents in **ready money**, and so much should
his mother, grandmother, kinsmen and friends, all the which were the
richest and wealthiest in Sparta. When the people heard what he said,
they marvelled much at the noble mind of this young king, and were
very glad of it, saying: that for three hundred years' space together,
the city of Sparta had not so worthy a king as he.

But Leonidas contrarily assayed with all his power he could to
resist him, thinking with himself, that if King Agis' purpose took
place, he should also be compelled [to contribute money], and yet he
should have no thanks, but King Agis [would]: because that all the
Spartans **indifferently** should be compelled to **make their goods in
common**, but the honour should be his only that first began it.

[The elders debated the proposal, but it was defeated by one vote.]

Part Two

Wherefore **Lysander**, who was yet in office, attempted to accuse
Leonidas by an ancient law, forbidding that none of the race of
Hercules should marry with any **strange** woman, nor beget children
of her, [because] he had married a woman [in] Asia, and had two
children by her; and afterwards being forsaken [by her], he returned
again into his country against his will, and so had possessed the
kingdom for lack of lawful heir.

So following his accusation in this manner, [Lysander persuaded]
Cleombrotus [the king's] son-in-law, being also of the king's blood,
to make title to the crown. Leonidas being afraid of **the success**

hereof, took sanctuary in the temple of **Juno, surnamed Chalceaecos,** and his daughter with him, who forsook her husband Cleombrotus. Leonidas then being cited to appear in person, and **making default, they deposed him,** and made Cleombrotus king.

In the meantime, Lysander's office [of ephor] expired, and the new ephors which succeeded him did deliver Leonidas again, and accused Lysander and Mandroclidas, because **against the law,** they had abolished all debts, and had again made new division of lands. When they saw that they were openly accused, they [proposed to] both the kings, that joining together, they should make the ephors' ordinances of no effect: declaring that their authority was only erected for the discord of the two kings, because they [the ephors] should give their voices unto that king that had the best judgement and reason, when the other would willfully withstand both right and reason. And therefore, that they two agreeing together, might lawfully do what they would, without controlment of any person: and that to resist the kings was a breaking of the law, [since] by right the ephors had no other privilege and authority, but to be judges and arbitrators between them, when there was any cause of **jar** or controversy.

Both the kings being carried away by this persuasion, went into the marketplace accompanied with their friends, plucked the ephors from their seats, and put others in their rooms, of the which Agesilaus was one. Furthermore, they armed a great number of young men, and opening the prisons, did set the prisoners at liberty: which made their adversaries afraid of them, [fearing] some great murder would have followed upon it; howbeit, no man had any hurt. For Agesilaus [was] bent to kill Leonidas, who fled unto the city of Tegea, and also laid men in wait for him by the way. King Agis, hearing of it, sent thither other friends of his in whom he put great confidence, and they did accompany Leonidas, and brought him safely unto the city of Tegea.

Thus their purpose taking effect, and no man contrarying them: one man only, Agesilaus, overthrew all, and dashed a noble Laconian law by a shameful **vice,** which was covetousness. For he, having the best lands of any man in the country, and owing a great sum of money besides, would neither pay his debts, nor let go his land. Wherefore he persuaded King Agis, that if he [Agis] went about to **[e]stablish both together,** he should raise a great uproar in the city, and withal, if he did first win them that were landed men, **preferring** at the beginning the cutting of debts only: then that they would easily and willingly also accept the law for partition of lands. Lysander was also of his opinion: whereby King Agis and he both were deceived by Agesilaus' subtlety. So they commanded all the creditors to bring their bonds, obligations, and bills of debt (which the Lacedaemonians do call *Claria*) into the marketplace, and there laying them on a heap together, they did set fire of them. When the **usurers** and creditors saw their writings obligatory afire, they departed thence with heavy hearts: but Agesilaus, mocking them, said he never saw a brighter fire in his life.

Narration and Discussion

Why was King Leonidas so resistant to Agis' proposals?

How (and why) did Agesilaus deceive Agis and Lysander?

If you were a creditor in Sparta, and you knew you would lose money if all debts were cancelled, would you be willing to accept the reforms for the sake of restoring honour and the old ways to the city?

Lesson Three

Introduction

In a passage between **Lessons Two** and **Three** (omitted for length), the Spartans demanded that the lands should be divided as they had agreed, but Agesilaus (the uncle of Agis) found reasons to delay this. At this time also, King Agis led an army to Corinth, to help prevent an invasion by the Aetolians, and "shewed himself in his counsel, then no rash, but a resolute and valiant man." But when Agis returned home, he found Sparta "in great broil and trouble."

Vocabulary

tallages and taxes...: government taxes

he made no account of the one [Cleombrotus]: he scoffed at him

his enemies: the enemies of Agesilaus were also the enemies of Agis

a humble suitor: Dryden says "a suppliant," someone making a plea

honest colour to excuse his fault: justification for his error

get him thence: go away from there

vainglory: selfish ambition

come by: entrap (Dryden)

beguile: deceive

incontinently: quickly

as if it had been judicially: as if things were proceeding lawfully

the commonwealth: the state, the government

soldiers which were strangers: foreign mercenaries

the Decade: a place of execution

manifest: obvious

Historic Occasions

243 B.C.: Agis led an army against Aratus at Corinth

242 B.C.: Leonidas was exiled

241 B.C.: the death of Agis

Reading

Part One

For Agesilaus at that time being one of the ephors, finding himself rid of the fear which before kept him under [some restraint]: cared not what injury or mischief he did to any citizen, so he might get money. For amongst other things, that very year he made them pay beyond all reason the **tallages and taxes due unto the commonwealth** for thirteen months, adding to the thirteenth month, above the ordinary time of the year. Wherefore perceiving every man hated him, and being afraid of them he had offended: he kept soldiers about him, armed with their swords, and so came down into the marketplace among them. And for the two kings, **he made no account of the one [Cleombrotus]**: but of the other, that was Agis, he seemed outwardly to make good account, rather for kindred's sake, than for his dignity of a king, and furthermore gave it out abroad, that he would also be one of the ephors the next year following.

Whereupon, **his enemies** speedily to prevent the danger, gathered force together and openly brought King Leonidas from Tegea, to restore him again to his kingdom. The people were glad to see that, because they were angry they had been mocked in that sort, for that the lands were not divided according unto promise. Furthermore, Hippomedon was so well-beloved for his valiantness [by] every man, that entreating the people for his father Agesilaus, he saved his life, and got him out of the city.

But [as] for the two kings, Agis took sanctuary in the temple of Juno Chalceaecos. And Cleombrotus the other king fled into the temple of Neptune: for it seemed that Leonidas being much more offended with him, did let King Agis alone, and went against him [Cleombrotus] with certain soldiers armed. Then he [Leonidas] sharply taunted him, that being his son-in-law, he had conspired against him to deprive him of his kingdom, and had driven him out of his country. But then Cleombrotus, not having a word to say, sat still, and made him no answer.

Whereupon his wife Chelonis, the daughter of Leonidas, who before was offended for the injury they did her father, and had left her husband Cleombrotus, that had usurped the kingdom from him, to serve her father in his adversity, and while he was in sanctuary took part with him also of his misery, and afterwards when he went unto the city of Tegea, wore blacks for sorrow, being offended with her husband: she contrarily then changing her anger with her husband's fortune and misery, became also **a humble suitor** with him, sitting down by him, and embracing him, having her two little sons on either side of them. All men wondering, and weeping for pity, to see the goodness and natural love of this lady, who shewing her mourning apparel, and hair of her head flaring about her eyes, bareheaded: she spake in this sort unto her father:

"O father mine, this sorrowful garment and countenance is not for pity of Cleombrotus, but hath long remained with me, lamenting sore your former misery and exile: but now, which of the two should I rather choose, either to continue a mourner in this pitiful state, seeing you again restored to your kingdom, having overcome your enemies: or else putting on my princely apparel, to see my husband slain, unto whom you married me as a maid? Who, if he cannot move you to take compassion of him, and to obtain mercy, by the tears of his wife and children: he shall then abide more bitter pain of his evil counsel, than that which you intend to make him suffer... And for my husband, if he had any reason to do that he did, I then took it from him, by taking your part, and protesting against him: and contrarily, yourself doth give him **honest colour to excuse his fault**, when he seeth in you the desire of the kingdom so great, that for the love thereof, you think it lawful to kill your sons-in-law, and also not to regard the children he hath gotten, for her sake."

Chelonis pitifully complaining in this sort, putting her face upon Cleombrotus' head, cast her swollen and blubbering eyes upon the standers-by.

Wherefore Leonidas after he had talked a little with his friends, he commanded Cleombrotus to **get him thence**, and to leave the city as an exile: and prayed his daughter for his sake to remain with him, and not to forsake her father, that did so dearly love her, as for her sake he had saved her husband's life. This notwithstanding, she would not yield to his request, but rising up with her husband, gave him one of his sons, and herself took the other in her arms: and then making her prayer before the altar of the goddess, she went as a banished woman away with her husband. And truly the example of her virtue was so famous, that if Cleombrotus' mind had not been too much blinded with **vainglory**, he had cause to think his exile far more happy, to enjoy the love of so noble a wife as he had, than for the kingdom which he possessed without her.

Part Two

Then Leonidas having banished King Cleombrotus out of the city, and removing the first ephors, had substituted other[s] in their place: he presently bethought him how he might craftily **come by** King Agis. First, he persuaded him to come out of the sanctuary, and to govern the kingdom safely with him, declaring unto him that his citizens had forgiven him all that was past, because they knew he was deceived, and subtly circumvented by Agesilaus' craft, being a young man, ambitious of honour. Agis would not leave the sanctuary for Leonidas' cunning persuasion, but mistrusted all that he said unto him: wherefore, Leonidas would no more **beguile** him with fair words.

But Amphares, Demochares, and Arcesilaus did oftentimes go to visit King Agis, and otherwhile also they got him out of the sanctuary with them unto the bath, and brought him back again into the temple, when he had bathed.

[*Amphares, having a personal grudge, betrayed Agis on the way back from the bath and had him taken to prison.*]

Then came Leonidas **incontinently** with a great number of soldiers, and beset the prison round about. The ephors went into the prison, and sent unto some of the Senate to come unto them, whom they knew to be of their mind: then they commanded Agis, **as if it had been judicially**, to give account of the alteration he had made in **the commonwealth**. The young man laughed at their hypocrisy. But Amphares told him that it was no laughing sport, and that he should pay for his folly.

Then another of the ephors seeming to deal more favourably with him, and to shew him a way how he might escape the condemnation for his fault: asked him, if he had not been enticed unto it by Agesilaus and Lysander. Agis answered, that no man compelled him, but that he only did it to follow the steps of the ancient Lycurgus, to bring the commonwealth unto the former estate of his grave ordinance and institution. Then the same senator asked him again, if he did not repent him of that he had done. The young man boldly answered him, that he would never repent him of so wise and virtuous an enterprise, though he ventured his life for it. Then they condemned him to death.

Demochares perceiving the sergeants durst not lay hold of him, and likewise that the **soldiers which were strangers**, did abhor to commit such a fact, contrary to the law of God and man, to lay violent hands upon the person of a king: he threatened and reviled them, and dragged Agis perforce into that place called **the Decade**.

Now the rumor ran straight through the city, that King Agis was taken, and a multitude of people were at the prison doors with lights and torches. Thither came also King Agis' mother and grandmother, shrieking out, and praying that the King of Sparta might yet be heard and judged by the people. For this cause, they hastened his death the sooner, and were afraid besides, lest the people in the night would take him out of their hands by force, if there came any more people thither.

Thus King Agis, being led to his death, spied a sergeant lamenting and weeping for him, unto whom he said: "Good fellow, I pray thee weep not for me, for I am honester man than they that so shamefully put me to death," and with those words he willingly put his head into the halter.

[The mother and grandmother of King Agis were put to death as well.]

This horrible murder being blown abroad in the city, and the three dead bodies also brought out of prison: the fear though it were great amongst the people, could not keep them back from apparent show of grief, and **manifest** hate against Leonidas and Amphares, thinking that there was never a more wicked and crueller fact committed in Sparta, since the Dorians came to dwell in Peloponnesus.

Narration and Discussion

If you had been Chelonis, the daughter of Leonidas, would you have stayed in Sparta with him, or gone into exile with your husband? Why do you think she made the choice she did?

How did Agis demonstrate courage during his trial?

Lesson Four

Introduction

In this lesson we meet Cleomenes, first as a young prince of Sparta, and then as king. Forced to marry the widow of Agis, he had the opportunity to hear the whole story from the inside out.

Vocabulary

vertuousest and best conditioned: Dryden: "well-conducted in her habits of life"

had not that shamefast modesty and lenity: Dryden: "not so scrupulous, circumspect, and gentle"

by compulsion also: if he had to, he would force them to reform

the preferment whereof: the bringing up of which

a young stripling: a boy

listed: desired

prove: test

lost his journey: wasted his time

finely: sarcastically

let: opposed, prevented

People

Sphaerus: a Stoic philosopher

Zenon Citian: founder of the Stoic school of philosophy

Historic Occasions

235 B.C.: the death of King Leonidas

229 B.C.: the Achaean League declared war against Sparta; Cleomenes was sent to capture the fort at Athaenium

Reading

Part One

Now Agis having suffered in this sort, Leonidas was not quick enough to take Archidamus his brother also, for he fled presently. Yet he brought Agis' wife out of her house by force, with a little boy she had by him, and married her unto his son Cleomenes, who was yet under age to marry: fearing lest this young lady should be bestowed elsewhere, being indeed a great heir, and of a rich house, and the daughter of Gylippus, called by her name Agiatis, besides that she was the fairest woman at that time in all Greece, and the **vertuousest and best conditioned**. Wherefore, for divers respects she prayed she might not be forced to it.

But now being at length married unto Cleomenes, she ever hated Leonidas to the death, and yet was a good and loving wife unto her young husband: who immediately after he was married unto her, fell greatly in fancy with her, and for compassion's sake (as it seemed) he thanked her for the love she bare unto her first husband, and for the loving remembrance she had of him: insomuch as he himself many times would fall in talk of it, and would be inquisitive how things had passed, taking great pleasure to hear of Agis' wise counsel and purpose. For Cleomenes was as desirous of honour, and had as noble a mind as Agis, and was born also to temperancy and moderation of life, as Agis in like manner was: howbeit, he **had not that shamefast modesty and lenity** which the other had, but was somewhat more stirring of nature, and readier to put any good matter in execution. So he thought it great honesty to bring the citizens if he could, to be contented to live after an honest sort: but contrarily, he thought it no dishonesty to bring them unto good life **by compulsion also**.

Furthermore, the manners of the citizens of Sparta, giving themselves over to idleness and pleasure, [he did not like] at all. [The king let everything take its own way, thankful if nobody gave him any disturbance, nor called him away from the enjoyment of his wealth and luxury. The public interest was neglected, and each man [was] intent upon his private gain.] And contrarily, it was not lawful for any man to speak for the exercises of the youth, for their education in temperancy, and for the restoring again of the equality of life, **the preferment whereof** was the only cause of the late death of Agis.

They say also, that Cleomenes, [when he was] **a young stripling**, had heard some disputation of philosophy, when the philosopher **Sphaerus**, of the country of Borysthenes, came to Lacedaemon, and lovingly stayed there to teach young men and children. He was one of the chiefest scholars of **Zenon Citian**, and delighted (as it seemed) in Cleomenes' noble mind, and had a great desire to prick him forward unto honour.

Part Two

Now Leonidas (the father of Cleomenes) being deceased, and he himself [Cleomenes] come unto the crown, finding that the citizens of Sparta at that time were very dissolute, that the rich men followed their pleasure and profit taking no care of the commonweal, that the poor men also for very want and need went with no good life and courage to the wars, neither cared for the bringing up of their children, and that he himself had but the name of a king, and the ephors the absolute authority to do what they **listed**: at his first coming to his kingdom, he determined to alter the whole state and government of the commonwealth.

Part Three

When King Leonidas was dead, Aratus began to invade the Arcadians, those specially that bordered upon the Argives: to **prove** how the Lacedaemonians would take it, making no account of Cleomenes, being but a young king, [who] had no experience of wars.

Thereupon the ephors sent Cleomenes unto Athaenium (a temple of Minerva hard by the city of Belbina), with an army to take it: because it was a passage and entry into the country of Laconia, howbeit the place at that time was in question betwixt the Megalopolitans and the Lacedaemonians. Cleomenes got it, and fortified it. Aratus making no complaint otherwise of the matter, stole out one night with his army to set upon the Tegeans and Orchomenians, hoping to have taken those cities by treason. But the traitors that were of his confederacy, their hearts failed them when they should have gone about it: so that Aratus returned, having **lost his journey**, thinking that this secret attempt of his was not discovered.

But Cleomenes **finely** wrote unto him, as [if he were] his friend, and asked him, whether [*Dryden: whither*] he had led his army by night: Aratus returned answer again, that understanding Cleomenes meant to fortify Belbina, he went forth with his army, thinking to have **let** him. Cleomenes wrote again unto him, and said he did believe that which he spake was true: howbeit he earnestly requested him, (if it were no trouble to him) to advertise him why he brought scaling ladders and lights after him. Aratus smiling at this mock, asked what this young man was. Democritus, [a Spartan exile], answered; "If thou hast any thing to do against the Lacedaemonians, thou hadst need make haste, before this young cockerel have on his spurs." [*Dryden uses a different metaphor: "begin before this young eagle's talons are grown."*]

Narration and Discussion

Describe the unexpected outcome of the marriage between Agiatis and Cleomenes.

What impression did General Aratus get of his enemy Cleomenes during these events?

Lesson Five

Introduction

Cleomenes continued to fight successfully against the **Achaean League** (see introductory notes), but wars are expensive, and he needed to convince the Spartans that it would be worthwhile in the end. After unsuccessfully attempting to bring back the brother of Agis, he realized that the real power lay with the five ephors.

Vocabulary

the borders of the Argives: the territory around Argos

he put a strong garrison into it: he fortified it with soldiers

resisting Cleomenes' enterprises: Cleomenes realized that his military agenda was unpopular, especially with the ephors, and particularly after Aratus seized Mantinea

unto whom the kingdom of right belonged...: Archidamus was the rightful hereditary king of the Eurypontids

one of the chiefest citizens for wealth and power: that is, Megistonus

furtherance: advancement of the scheme

wont: accustomed

took the cities of Heraea and Alsea, etc.: kept the army [made up largely of his non-supporters] very busy

strangers: mercenary soldiers

imported his intent etc.: told his plan to those he trusted

commonwealth: a state, or, often, a group of states working together under one leadership

People

Megistonus / Megistonous: he was not the father-in-law of Cleomenes but his stepfather

Lysiadas: more commonly spelled **Lydiadas**.

Historic Occasions

226 B.C.: the Battle of Mount Lycaeum

Reading

Part One

Then Cleomenes being in the field in the country of Arcadia, with a few horsemen and three hundred footmen only: the ephors [*back in Sparta*] being afraid of wars, sent for him to return again. His back was no sooner turned, obeying their commandment: but Aratus suddenly took the city of Caphyes. Thereupon, the ephors incontinently sent Cleomenes back again with his army, and [the Spartans] took the fort of Methydrium, and burnt **the borders of the Argives**.

The Achaeans came against him with an army of twenty thousand footmen, and a thousand horsemen, led by Aristomachus. Cleomenes met with them by the city of Palantium, and offered battle. But Aratus, quaking at the hardiness of this young man, would not suffer Aristomachus to hazard battle, but went his way, derided by the Achaeans, and despised by the Lacedaemonians: who in all were not above five thousand fighting men. Cleomenes' courage being now lift[ed] up, and bravely speaking to his citizens: he [reminded] them of a saying of one of their ancient kings, that the Lacedaemonians never inquired what number their enemies were, but where they were.

Shortly after, the Achaeans making war with the Elians, Cleomenes was sent to aid them, and met with the army of the Achaeans by the mountain Lycaeum as they were in their return. He, setting upon them, gave them the overthrow, slew a great number of them, and took many also prisoners, [so] that the rumour ran through Greece, how Aratus [him]self was slain. Aratus, wisely taking the occasion which this victory gave him, went straight to the city of Mantinea, and taking it upon a sudden, when no man knew of his coming, **he put a strong garrison into it**.

Part Two

Now the Lacedaemonians' hearts failing them, and **resisting Cleomenes' enterprises**, overwearying them with wars: he went about to send for Archidamus, King Agis' brother, being then at Messena, **unto whom the kingdom of right belonged by the**

other house, supposing that he should easily weaken the power of the ephors, by the authority of the two kings, if both of them joined together. Which when the murderers of King Agis understood, being afraid that Archidamus returning from exile, he would be revenged of them: they secretly received him into the city, [and joined in bringing him home, and presently after murdered him. Whether Cleomenes was against it, as Phylarchus thinks, or whether he was persuaded by his friends, or let him fall into their hands, is uncertain; however, they were most blamed, as having forced his consent.]

Nevertheless, [Cleomenes] holding still his first determination, to alter the state of the **commonwealth** of Sparta, as soon as possible: he so fed the ephors with money, that he brought them to be contented [that] he should make war. He had also won many other citizens by the means of his mother Cratesiclea, who [spared no cost and was very zealous to promote her son's ambition; and though of herself she had no inclination to marry, yet for his sake she accepted, as her husband, **one of the chiefest citizens for wealth and power**].

So Cleomenes leading his army into the field, won a place within the territory of Megalopolis, called Leuctra. The Achaeans also quickly came to their aid, led by Aratus: they straight fought a battle by the city [it]self, where Cleomenes had the worst on the one side of his army. Howbeit Aratus would not suffer the Achaeans to follow them, because of bogs and quagmires, but sounded the retreat. But **Lysiadas**, a Megalopolitan, being angry withal, caused the horsemen he had about him to follow the chase, who pursued so fiercely, that they came amongst vines, walls, and ditches, where he was driven to disperse his men, and yet could not get out. Cleomenes perceiving it, sent the light horsemen of the Tarentins and Cretans against him: of whom Lysiadas, valiantly fighting, was slain.

Then the Lacedaemonians, being courageous for this victory, came with great cries; and giving a fierce charge upon the Achaeans, overthrew their whole army, and slew a marvellous number of them. But yet Cleomenes, at their request, suffered them to take up the dead bodies of their men to bury them. For Lysiadas' corpse, he caused it to be brought unto him, and putting a purple robe upon it, and a crown on his head, sent it in this array unto the very gates of the city of Megalopolis.

Part Three

[Cleomenes, being very much elated by this success], persuaded himself that if he might once come to [e]stablish the affairs of the **commonwealth** at Sparta to his mind, he might then easily overcome the Achaeans. [He persuaded] **his father-in-law Megistonus** that it was necessary to take away the authority of the ephors, and to make division of the lands among the Spartans, and then being brought to equality, to encourage them to recover the empire of Greece again unto the Lacedaemonians, which their predecessors before them held and enjoyed. Megistonus granting his good will and **furtherance**, joined two or three of his friends more unto him.

It chanced at that time that one of the ephors, lying in the temple of Pasiphae, had a marvellous dream in the night. For he thought he saw but one chair standing where the ephors did use to sit to give audience, and that the other four which were **wont** to be there, were taken away: and that marvelling at it, he heard a voice out of the temple that said, that was the best for Sparta. He declaring this dream the next morning unto Cleomenes, it somewhat troubled him [Cleomenes] at the first, thinking that he [the ephor] came to feel him, for that he had heard some inkling of his intent [to remove the ephors]. But when he persuaded himself that the other meant good faith, and lied not unto him, being bolder than before, he went forward with his purpose, and taking with him unto the camp all those Spartans which he suspected to be against his enterprise, he went and **took the cities of Heraea and Alsea, confederates of the Achaeans, and victualed Orchomena, and went and camped before the city of Mantinea.** In fine, he so wearied and overharried the Lacedaemonians by long journeys, that at length they besought him he would let them remain in Arcadia, to repose themselves there.

In the meantime, Cleomenes with his **strangers** which he had hired, returned again unto Sparta. [He] **imported his intent by the way unto them he trusted best**, and marched at his own ease, that he might take the ephors at supper. When he came near unto the city, he sent Euryclidas before, into the hall of the ephors, as though he brought them news out of the camp from him. After him, he sent also Thericion and Phoebis, and two other[s] that had been brought up with him, whom the Lacedaemonians called the Samothracians, taking with them a few soldiers. Now whilst Euryclidas was talking with the ephors, they also came in upon them with the swords drawn, and did set upon the ephors. Agesilaus was hurt first of all, and falling down, made as though he had been slain, but by little and little he crept out of the hall, and got secretly into a chapel consecrated unto Fear, the which was wont ever to be kept shut, but then by chance was left open: when he was come in, he shut the door fast to him. The other four of the ephors were slain presently, and above ten more besides, which came to defend them. Furthermore, for them that sat still and stirred not, they killed not a man of them, neither did keep any man that was desirous to go out of the city: but moreover, they pardoned Agesilaus, who came the next morning out of the Chapel of Fear.

Amongst the Lacedaemonians in the city of Sparta, there are not only temples of Fear and Death, but also of Laughter, and of many other such passions of the mind. They do worship Fear, not as other spirits and devils that are hurtful: but because they are persuaded, that nothing preserveth a **commonwealth** better than fear.

Narration and Discussion

"Nevertheless, [Cleomenes] holding still his first determination, to alter the state of the commonwealth of Sparta, as soon as possible: he so fed the ephors with money, that he brought them to be contented [that] he should make war." Why did Cleomenes' plan for a rejuvenated city depend on his continuing to fight the Achaeans?

"Nothing preserveth a **commonwealth** better than fear." Do you agree?

Lesson Six

Introduction

The Spartans were finding their old groove again, from the education of children to the re-institution of black broth and brown bread. The Achaeans, looking on, assumed that all the reforms had been enacted by force, and that Sparta must be on the verge of revolting against Cleomenes; but they were wrong.

Vocabulary

fourscore: eighty

plagues of the commonwealth: state troubles

make all his goods common: put his money into the public treasury

father-in-law: see previous note

pike: a *sarissa* or long spear, used in the Macedonian phalanx formation

target: shield

the ancient Laconian discipline: see introductory notes

he durst not: he dared not

late: recent

May-game: frivolous amusement

hardly: severely

board being taken up: table being removed after the meal

People

Sphaerus the philosopher: see **Lesson Four**

Reading

Part One

The next morning Cleomenes banished, by trumpet, **fourscore** citizens of Sparta, and overthrew all the chairs of the ephors but one only, the which he reserved for himself to sit in to give audience. Then calling the people to council, he [gave them a history lesson]:

> [He reminded them] that Lycurgus had joined the senators with the kings, and how the city had been governed a long time by them, without help of any other officers. Notwithstanding, afterwards the city

having great wars with the Messenians, the kings
being always employed in that war, whereby they
could not attend the affairs of the commonwealth at
home, did choose certain of their friends to sit in
judgment in their steads to determine controversies
of laws which were called ephors, and did govern
long time as the kings' ministers, howbeit that
afterwards, by little and little, they took upon them
absolute government by themselves [and abused
that power]...

Cleomenes continued his speech:

And therefore, if it had been possible to have
banished all these **plagues of the
commonwealth** out of Sparta, brought from
foreign nations (pleasures, pastimes, money, debts,
and usuries, poverty and riches), he [Cleomenes]
might then have esteemed himself the happiest king
that ever was, if like a good physician he had cured
his country of that infection, without grief or
sorrow. But in that he was constrained to begin with
blood, he [would] follow Lycurgus' example: who
being neither king nor other magistrate, but a
private citizen only, taking upon him the authority
of the king, boldly came into the marketplace with
force and armed men, and made King Charilaus
that then reigned, so afraid, that he was driven to
take sanctuary in one of the temples.

But [King Charilaus] being a prince of a noble
nature, and loving the honour of his country: took
part with Lycurgus, adding to his advice and
counsel, for the alteration of the state of the
government of the **commonwealth**, which he did
confirm. Hereby then it appeareth, that Lycurgus
saw it was a hard thing to alter the commonwealth
without force and fear; the which he [Cleomenes],
notwithstanding, had used with as great modesty
and discretion, as might be possible, banishing
them that were against the profit and wealth of
Lacedaemon, giving all the lands of the country also

to be equally divided amongst them, and setting all men clear that were in debt.

And furthermore, that he would make a choice and proof of the strangers, to make them free citizens of Sparta, whom he knew to be honest men, thereby to defend their city the better by force of arms.

Then he began first himself to **make all his goods common**, and [afterwards] Megistonus his **father-in-law**, and consequently all his other friends [did the same]. Then he caused the lands also to be divided, and ordained every banished man a part, whom he himself had exiled, promising that he would receive them again into the city, when he had established all things.

Part Two

So when he had replenished the number of the citizens of Sparta, with the choicest honest men their neighbours: he made four thousand footmen well armed, and taught them to use their **pikes** with both hands, instead of their darts with one hand, and to carry their **targets** with a good strong handle, and not buckled with a leather thong. Afterwards he took order for the education of children, and to restore **the ancient Laconian discipline** again: and did all these things in manner by the help of **Sphaerus the philosopher**. Insomuch as he had quickly set up again schoolhouses for children, and also brought them to the older order of diet: and all but a very few, without compulsion, were willing to fall to their old institution of life. [And, that the name of monarch might give them no jealousy, he made Euclidas, his brother, partner in the throne; and that was the only time that Sparta had two kings of the same family.]

Furthermore, understanding that the Achaeans and Aratus were of opinion that **he durst not** come out of Lacedaemon, for fear to leave it in peril of revolting, because of the **late** change and alteration in the commonwealth: he thought it an honourable attempt of him, to make his enemies see the readiness and goodwill of his army. Thereupon he invaded the territories of the **Megalopolitans**, and brought away a great prey and booty, after he had done great hurt unto his enemies. Then having taken certain players and minstrels that came from Messina, he set up a stage within the enemy's country, [offering a prize] of forty minas for the victor, and sat a whole day to look upon them, [not for the] pleasure he took in the sight of it, but more to despite the enemies withal, in making them see how much he was stronger than they, to make such a **May-game** in their own country, in despite of them.

For of all the armies otherwise of the Grecians, or kings in all Greece, there was no army only but his, that was without players, minstrels, fools and jugglers: for his camp only was clean of such rabble and foolery, and all the young men fell to some exercise of their bodies, and the old men also to teach them. And if they chanced to have any vacant time, then they would pleasantly be merry with [one another, diverting themselves with their native jests]. And what profit they got by that kind of exercise, we have written it at large in Lycurgus' *Life*. But of all these things, the king himself was their schoolmaster and example; [he was a living pattern of temperance before every man's eyes; and his course of living was neither more stately, nor more expensive, nor in any way more pretentious, than that of his people. And this was a considerable advantage to him in his designs on Greece]. For the Grecians having cause of suit and negotiation with other kings and princes, did not wonder so much at the pomp and riches [of those kings], as they did abhor and detest their pride and insolency: so disdainfully they would answer them that had to do with them. But contrarily, when they went unto Cleomenes, who was a king in name and deed as they were, finding no purple robes nor stately mantles, nor rich embroidered beds, nor a prince to be spoken to but by messengers, gentlemen ushers, and supplications, and yet with great ado: and seeing him also come plainly apparelled unto them, with a good countenance, and courteously answering the matters they came for: he thereby did marvellously win their hearts and goodwills, that when they returned home, they said he only was the worthy king that came of the race of Hercules.

[His common everyday's meal was in an ordinary room, very sparing, and after the Laconic manner; and when he entertained ambassadors, or strangers, two more couches were added, and a little better dinner provided by his servants]; not with pastry and conserves, but with more store of meat, and some better wine than ordinary. For he one day reproved one of his friends, that bidding strangers to supper he gave them nothing but black broth, and brown bread only, according to their Laconian manner. "Nay," said he, "we may not use strangers so **hardly** after our manner."

The **board being taken up**, another little table was brought with three feet, whereupon they set a bowl of copper full of wine, [two silver bowls, which held about a pint apiece, (and) a few silver cups, of which he that pleased might drink, but wine was not urged on any of the guests]. Furthermore, there was no sport, nor any pleasant song, to make the company merry, for it needed not. For Cleomenes [him]self would entertain them with some pretty questions, or pleasant tale: whereby, as his talk was not severe and without pleasure, so was it also pleasant without insolency. For he was of opinion, that to win men by gifts or money, as other kings and princes did, was [dishonest and artificial]: but to seek their good wills by courteous means, and pleasantries, and therewith to mean good faith, [was that which] he thought most fit and honourable for a prince. For this was his mind, that there was no other difference betwixt a friend and hireling: but that the one is won with money, and the other with civility and good entertainment [*Dryden: character and conversation*].

Narration and Discussion

In Part One, why was Cleomenes able to enact the reforms (in a seemingly short while) that Agis had proposed but been unable to carry out?

What do the dinner-party descriptions show about the character of Cleomenes?

Lesson Seven

Introduction

With his increasing military success, Cleomenes began to demand more concessions from those he had defeated. When he suddenly became too ill to attend a parliament with the Achaeans, Aratus took advantage of the lull to suggest that they should ask for help (once again) from Macedon. But the Achaeans, exasperatingly, seemed to prefer the prospect of being ruled by Cleomenes.

Vocabulary

dyet: assembly or parliament of the leaders. (**Dyet** is also spelled **diet**, as in the famous Diet of Worms.in 1521 A.D.)

proroguing: postponing

rotten man, consumed away: Antigonus was suffering from tuberculosis

indued: endowed; gifted

without: outside

with a flea in his ear: a lovely expression with meanings that can vary. Here it means "with a reprimand."

Historic Occasions

226 B.C.: the Mantineans asked for help against the Achaean League, and the Spartans fought the Achaeans at Dymes/Dyme

Reading

Part One

The first therefore that received King Cleomenes into their city, were the Mantinians, who opened him the gates in the night, and helping him to drive out the garrison of the Achaeans, they yielded themselves unto him. But he referring them to the use and government of their own laws and liberty, departed from thence the same day, and went unto the city of Tegea. Shortly after, he compassed about Arcadia, and came unto Pheres in Arcadia, [intending] either to give the Achaeans battle, or to bring Aratus out of favour with the people, for that he had suffered him [Cleomenes] to spoil and destroy their country. (Hyperbatas was at that time general of the Achaeans, but Aratus did bear all the sway and authority.)

Then the Achaeans coming into the field with all their people armed, and encamping by the city of Dymes, near unto the temple of Hecatombaeum. [Cleomenes came up, and thinking it not advisable to pitch (his camp) between Dymes, a city of the enemies, and the camp of the Achaeans, he boldly dared the Achaeans, and forced them to a battle], overthrew them, made them flee, and slew a great number in the field, and took many of them also prisoners.

Departing from thence, he went and set upon the city of Langon, and drove the garrison of the Achaeans out of it, and restored the city again unto the Elians.

The Achaeans [were] then in very hard state. Aratus, [who] of custom was wont to be their general (or at the least once in two years), refused now to take the charge, [although] the Achaeans did specially pray and entreat him: the which was an ill act of him, to let another steer the rudder, in so dangerous a storm and tempest. [Cleomenes at first proposed fair and easy conditions by his ambassadors to the Achaeans, but afterwards he sent others, and required the chief command to be settled upon him]; and that for all other matters he would deal reasonably with them, and presently deliver them up their towns and prisoners again, which he had taken of theirs. The Achaeans being glad of peace with these conditions, wrote unto Cleomenes that he should come unto the city of Lerna, where the **dyet** and general assembly should be kept to consult thereupon. It chanced then that Cleomenes marching thither, being very hot, drank cold water, and fell of such a bleeding withal, that his voice was taken from him, and he almost stifled. Wherefore he sent the Achaeans their chiefest prisoners home again, **proroguing** the parliament till another time, and returned back to Lacedaemon.

[This ruined the affairs of Greece, which was just beginning in some sort to recover from its disasters, and to show some capability of delivering itself from the insolence and rapacity of the Macedonians.] For Aratus, either for that he trusted not Cleomenes, or for that he was afraid of his power, or that he otherwise envied his honour and prosperity, to see him risen to such incredible greatness in so short a time, and thinking it also too great shame and dishonour to him, to suffer this young man in a moment to deprive him of his great honour and power which he had possessed so long time, by the space of thirty years together, ruling all Greece: first, he sought by force to terrify the Achaeans, and to make them break off from this peace. But in fine, finding that they little regarded his threats, and that he could not prevail with them, for that they were afraid of Cleomenes' valiantness and courage, whose request they thought reasonable, for that he sought but to restore Peloponnesus into her former ancient estate again: he fell then into a practise far unhonest for a Grecian, very infamous for himself, but most dishonourable for the former noble acts he had done.

For [Aratus] brought Antigonus into Greece, and filled the country of Peloponnesus with Macedonians, whom he himself in his youth had driven thence, [when he] had taken from them the castle of Corinth. And furthermore, fleeing them that were contented with brown bread, and with the plain coarse capes of the Lacedaemonians, and that went about to take away riches (which was the chiefest matter they did accuse Cleomenes for) and to provide for the poor: he went and put himself and all Achaea into the crown and diadem, the purple robe, and proud imperious commandments of the Macedonians, fearing lest men should think that Cleomenes could command him. Furthermore his folly was such that, having garlands of flowers on his head, he did sacrifice unto Antigonus, and sing songs in praise of his honour, as if he had been a god, where he was but **a rotten man, consumed away**.

This that we have written of Aratus (who was **indued** with many noble virtues, and a worth Grecian) is not so much to accuse him, as to make us see the frailty and weakness of man's nature: the which, though it have never so excellent virtues, cannot yet bring forth such perfect fruit, but that it hath ever some maim and blemish.

Part Two

Now, when the Achaeans were met again in the city of Argos, to hold the session of their parliament [which had been] **prorogued**, and Cleomenes also being come from Tegea, to be at that parliament: every man was in hope of good peace. But Aratus then, who was agreed before of the chiefest articles of the capitulations with Antigonus, fearing that Cleomenes by fair words or force would bring the people to grant that [which] he desired: sent to let him understand, that he should but come himself alone into the city, and for safety of his person, they would give him three hundred hostages: or otherwise, if he would not leave his army, that then they would give him audience **without** the city, in the place of exercises, called Cyllarabium. Then Cleomenes had heard their answer, he told them that they had done him wrong: for they should have advertised him of it before he had taken his journey, and not now when he was almost hard at their gates, to send him back again, **with a flea in his ear.**

Thereupon he wrote a letter unto the council of the Achaeans, altogether full of complaints against Aratus. On the other side also, Aratus in his oration to the council, [spoke violently] against Cleomenes. Thereupon Cleomenes departing with speed, sent a herald to proclaim wars against the Achaeans, not in the city of Argos, but in the city of Aegion, as Aratus writeth, meaning to set upon them being unprovided. Hereupon all Achaea was in an uproar: for divers cities did presently revolt against the Achaeans, because the common people hoped after the division of lands, and the discharging of the debts. The noble men also in many places were offended with Aratus, because he practised to bring the Macedonians into the country of Peloponnesus.

Cleomenes, therefore, hoping well for all these respects, brought his army into Achaea, and at his first coming took the city of Pallena, and drove out the garrison of the Achaeans: and after that, won also the cities of Pheneum, and Pentilium.

Narration and Discussion

"This that we have written of Aratus...is not so much to accuse him, as to make us see the frailty and weakness of man's nature: the which, though it have never so excellent virtues, cannot yet bring forth such perfect fruit, but that it hath ever some maim and blemish." Does this help to explain Plutarch's aim in writing biographies?

Lesson Eight

Introduction

If you have read Plutarch's *Life of Pyrrhus*, you will remember his great battle in the city of Argos: soldiers, citizens, and elephants every which way, trying to come in and trying to get out. The impossibility of conquering Argos was, therefore, legendary: but Cleomenes managed it. The Spartans' rediscovered power made them enough of a threat that Aratus gave up trying to fight them; but not before sending Antigonus and his very powerful Macedonian army marching in their direction.

Vocabulary

hard to: close to

ill to come unto: hard to access

garrison: military troops

kept indifferently: held equally

provided for corn: brought enough food supplies

quietly: Dryden says "merrily"

promontory: headland, high point

tarried not his coming: didn't wait for him to arrive

advertisement hereof: news of this

attended: waited for

phalanx: a tight battle formation used by the Macedonians

Reading

Part One

Now the Achaeans fearing some treason in Corinth and Sycione, sent certain horsemen out of the city of Argos, to keep those cities. The Argives in the meantime, attending the celebration of the feast at the Nemean games, Cleomenes thinking (which fell out true) that if he went to Argos, he should find the city full of people that were come to see the feasts and games, and that assailing them upon the sudden, he should put them in a marvellous fear: [he] brought his army in the night **hard to** the walls of the city of Argos, and at his first coming won a place they call Aspis, a very strong place above the theater, and **ill to come unto**. The Argives were so amazed at it, that no man would take upon him to defend the city, but received Cleomenes' **garrison**, and gave him twenty hostages, promising thenceforth to be true confederates unto the Lacedaemonians, under his charge and conduct. The which doubtless won him great fame, and increased his power: [because] the ancient kings of Lacedaemon, could never before with any policy or device, win the city of Argos. For [even] King Pyrrhus, one of the valiantest and [most] warlike prince[s] that ever was, entering the city of Argos by force, could not keep it, but was slain there, and the most part of his army: whereby, every man wondered greatly at the diligence and counsel of Cleomenes.

And where every man did mock him before, when Cleomenes said that he would follow Solon and Lycurgus, in making the citizens' goods common, and discharging all debts: they were then clearly persuaded that he only was the cause and mean of that great change, which they saw in the courage of the Spartans: who were before so weak and out of heart, that [previously] they having no courage to defend themselves, the Aetolians entering Laconia, with an army, took away at one time, fifty thousand slaves. Whereupon an old man of Sparta pleasantly said at that time, that their enemies had done them a great pleasure, to rid their country of Laconia of such a rabble of rascals.

Shortly after, they being entered again into the former ancient discipline of Lycurgus, as if Lycurgus [him]self had been alive to have trained them unto it: they shewed themselves very valiant, and obedient also unto their magistrates, whereby they recovered again the commandment of all Greece, and the country also of Peloponnesus. After Cleomenes had taken the city of Argos, the cities also of Cleones and Phliunta did yield themselves unto him. Aratus in the meantime remained at Corinth, and there did busily accuse them which were suspect to favour the Lacedaemonians. But when news was brought him that Argos was taken, and that he perceived also the city of Corinth did lean unto Cleomenes' part, and drave away the Achaeans: he then calling the people to council in Corinth, secretly stole to one of the gates of the city, and causing his horse to be brought unto him, took his back, and galloped for life unto the city of Sicyone.

When the Corinthians heard of it, they took [to] their horsebacks also, striving who should be there soonest, and posted in such haste unto Cleomenes at the city of Argos, that many of them (as Aratus writeth) killed their horses by the way. Howbeit Cleomenes was very much offended with them, for that they had let him [Aratus] [e]scape their hands. But Aratus saith further [*in his writings*], that **Megistonus** came unto him from Cleomenes, and offered him a great sum of money to deliver him the castle of Corinth, wherein there was a great garrison of the Achaeans. But he answered again, that things were not in his power, but rather that he was subject to their power.

Part Two

Now Cleomenes departing from the city of Argos, overcame the Troezenians, the Epidaurians, and the Hermionians. After that, he came unto Corinth, and presently entrenched the castle there round about, and sending for Aratus' friends and factors, commanded them to keep [Aratus'] house and goods carefully for him, and sent Tritymallus Messenian again unto [Aratus], to pray him to be contented that the castle might be **kept indifferently** betwixt the Achaeans and Lacedaemonians, promising him privately to double the pension that King Ptolemy gave him. But Aratus refusing it, sent his son unto Antigonus with other hostages, and persuaded the Achaeans to deliver up the castle of Corinth, unto Antigonus' hands. [Upon this Cleomenes invaded the territory of the Sicyonians, and by a decree of the Corinthians, accepted Aratus' estate as a gift.]

Part Three

Now Antigonus in the meantime, [was passing] the mountain of Gerania with a great power. Cleomenes determined not to fortify the isthmus or strait of Peloponnesus, but [the mountains called Onea]; determining to keep every one of them against the Macedonians, with intent to consume them rather by time, than to fight a battle with an army, so good soldiers and well trained as they were. Cleomenes following this determination, did put Antigonus to great trouble, because he had not in time **provided for corn**: and could not win the passage also by force, for that Cleomenes kept it with such guard and soldiers. Then Antigonus stealing secretly into the haven of Lechaeum, he was stoutly repulsed, and lost a number of his men: whereupon Cleomenes and his men, being courageous for this victory, went **quietly** to supper.

Antigonus on the other side fell into despair, to see himself brought by necessity into such hard terms. Wherefore he determined to go to the [**promontory** at the] temple of Juno, and from thence to pass his army by sea into the city of Sicyone, which required a long time, and great preparation. But the same night there came some of Aratus' friends of the Argives, who coming from Argos by sea, brought news that the Argives were rebelled against Cleomenes. The practiser of this rebellion was one Aristototeles, who easily brought the people unto it, [who] were already offended with Cleomenes, [because he] had promised to pass a law for the clearing of debts, but performed it not according to their expectation.

Wherefore, Aratus with a thousand five hundred men which **Antigonus** gave him, went by sea unto Epidaurum. Howbeit Aristoteles [the leader of the rebellion] **tarried not his coming**, but taking them of the city with him, went and besieged the garrison of the Lacedaemonians within the castle, being aided by Timoxenus, with the Achaeans that came from Siciyone.

Cleomenes receiving **advertisement hereof**, about the second watch of the night, sent for Megistonus in haste, and commanded him in anger speedily to go and [set things right at Argos. Megistonus had passed his word for the Argives' loyalty, and had persuaded him not to banish the suspected.] So sending him away forthwith with two thousand men, he **attended** Antigonus, and comforted the Corinthians the best he could: advertising them that it was but a little mutiny of a few, that chanced in the city of Argos.

[But when Megistonus, entering Argos, was slain, and the garrison could scarce hold out, and frequent messengers came to Cleomenes for succours], Cleomenes then being afraid that the enemies having taken Argos, would stop his way to return back into his country, who having opportunity safely to spoil Laconia, and also to besiege the city [it]self of Sparta, that had but a few men to defend it: he departed with his army from Corinth. Immediately after came Antigonus, and took it from him, and put a strong garrison into it.

When Cleomenes came before the city of Argos, he scaled the walls, and breaking [into the] Aspis, entered into the city, and joined with his garrison there, which yet resisted the Achaeans: and [he] taking other parts of the same also, assaulted the walls; [and his Cretan archers cleared the streets]. [But when he saw Antigonus with his **phalanx** descending from the mountains into the plain, and the horse on all sides entering the city, he thought it impossible to maintain his post; and, gathering] all his men together, and safely going down by the walls, retired without loss of any man.

So, when in short time he had conquered much, and had almost won all within Peloponnesus: in shorter space also, he lost all again. For, of [those] that were in his camp, some did presently forsake him: others also immediately after surrendered up [their] towns unto Antigonus.

Cleomenes being thus oppressed with the fortune of war, when he came back to Tegea with the rest of his army, news came to him in the night from Lacedaemon, which grieved him as much as the loss of all his conquests: for he was advertised of the death of his wife Agiatis, whom he loved so dearly, that in the midst of his chiefest prosperity and victories, he made often journeys to Sparta to see her. It could not be but a marvellous grief unto Cleomenes, who being a young man, had lost so virtuous and fair a young lady, so dearly beloved of him: and yet he gave not place unto his sorrow, neither did grief overcome his noble courage, but he used the selfsame voice, apparel, and countenance, that he did before.

Then taking order with his private captains about his affairs, and having provided also for the safety of the Tegeans: he went the next morning by break of day unto Sparta. After he had privately lamented the sorrow of his wife's death, with his mother and children, he presently bent his mind again to public causes.

Narration and Discussion

How was it that the Spartans, who had recently had so much success, were beaten by the Macedonians? Why did Cleomenes choose not to try to defend Argos against them?

Cleomenes was now at a difficult point, both personally and as the ruler and general of Sparta. What do you think would be his next move? If you could advise Cleomenes, what would you say to him?

Lesson Nine

Introduction

Sparta was not powerful enough to stand against Macedonia alone, so Cleomenes asked for help from Egypt. King Ptolemy didn't require much in return: only Cleomenes' mother and son as hostages. At the same time, the Macedonians were attacking the borders of Spartan territory. It seemed that all would be lost; but "then there fell into his mind a marvellous great enterprise, unlooked for of every man."

Vocabulary

in pledge: as hostages

expedient: good, beneficial

he did manumize all the helots etc.: The helots were the lowest class in ancient Sparta, similar to serfs. By encouraging them to buy their freedom, Cleomenes raised enough money to outfit his army.

nothing was more requisite than celerity: speed was essential

fair and softly: at a leisurely pace

Reading

Part One

Now Cleomenes had sent unto Ptolemy, king of Egypt, who had promised him aid, but upon demand to have his mother and children **in pledge**. So he was a long time before he would for shame make his mother privy unto it, and went oftentimes of purpose to let her understand it: but when he first came, he had not the heart to break it to her.

She first suspecting a thing, asked Cleomenes' friends, if her son had not somewhat to say unto her, that he durst not utter. [At last, Cleomenes venturing to tell her], she fell a-laughing, and told him: "Why, how cometh it to pass, that thou hast kept it thus long, and wouldst not tell me? Come, come," said she, "put me straight into a ship, and send me whither thou wilt, that this body of mine may do some good unto my country, before crooked age consume[s] my life without profit."

Then all things being prepared for the journey, they went by land, accompanied with the army, [to] Taenarus. Where Cratesiclea being ready to embark, she took Cleomenes aside into the temple of

Neptune, and embracing and kissing him, perceiving that his heart yearned for sorrow of her departure, she said unto him: "O King of Laecedaemon, let no man see for shame, when we come out of the temple, that we have wept and dishonoured Sparta. For that only is in our power, and for the rest, as it pleaseth the gods, so let it be." When she had spoken these words, and fashioned her countenance again: she went then to take her ship, with a little son of Cleomenes, and commanded the master of the ship to hoist sail.

Now when she was arrived in Egypt, and understood that King Ptolemy received ambassadors from Antigonus, and were in talk to make peace with him: and hearing also that Cleomenes [though the Achaeans invited and urged him to an agreement, was afraid, for her sake, to come to any, without Ptolemy's consent]; she wrote unto him, that he should not spare to do anything that should be **expedient** for the honour of Sparta, without fear of displeasing Ptolemy, or for regards of an old woman and a young boy. Such was the noble mind of this worthy lady in her son Cleomenes' adversity.

Part Two

Furthermore, Antigonus having taken the city of Tegea, and sacked the other cities of Orchomenum, and Mantinea: Cleomenes seeing himself brought to defend the borders only of Laconia, **he did manumize all the helots, paying five Attica minas a man**. With that money he made the sum of five hundred talents, and armed two thousand of these freed slaves after the Macedonian fashion to fight against the Leucaspides ("the white shields"); and then there fell into his mind a marvellous great enterprise, unlooked for of every man.

The city of Megalopolis at that time being as great as Sparta, and having the aid of the Achaeans and Antigonus at hand (whom the Achaeans as it seemed had brought in, chiefly at the request of the Megalopolitans); Cleomenes determining to sack this city, and knowing that to bring it to pass, **nothing was more requisite than celerity:** he commanded his soldiers to victual themselves for five days, and marching with the choice of all his army towards Selasia, as though he had meant to have spoiled the Argives, suddenly turning from thence, he invaded the country of the Megalopolitans, and supping by Roetium, went straight by Elicunta unto the city.

When he was come near unto it, he sent Panteas before with

speed, with two bands of the Lacedaemonians, and commanded him to take a certain piece of the wall between two towers, which he knew was not kept nor guarded: and he followed him also with the rest of his army coming on **fair and softly**. When Panteas came thither, finding not only that place of the wall without guard or watch which Cleomenes had told him of, but also the most part of that side without defence: he took some part of the wall at his first coming, and manned it, and overthrew another piece of it also, putting them all to the sword that did defend it, and then came Cleomenes, and [he] was within the city with his army, before the Megalopolitans knew of his coming.

At length, the citizens understanding that the city was taken, some fled in haste, conveying such light things as came to hand, in so great a fear: and the others also arming themselves, ran together to resist the enemies. But though they valiantly fought to repulse them out of the city, and yet prevailed not: they gave the rest leisure there to flee and save themselves, so that there remained not behind, above a thousand men. For all the rest were led with their wives and children, into the city of Messena. The most part of them also that fought with the enemies, saved themselves, and very few were taken, the chiefest whereof were Lysandridas, and Thearidas, the noblest persons that were amongst the Megalopolitans: wherefore when the soldiers had taken them, they brought them unto Cleomenes.

Lysandridas, when he saw Cleomenes a good way off, cried out aloud unto him: "O King of Lacedaemon, this day thou hast an occasion offered thee to do a more famous princely act, than that which thou hast already done, and that will make thy name also more glorious."

Cleomenes musing what he would request: "Well," quoth he, "what is that thou requirest? One thing I will tell thee beforehand, thou shalt not make me restore your city to you again."

"Yet," quoth Lysandridas, "let me request thus much then, that ye do not destroy it, but rather replenish it with friends and confederates, which hereafter will be true and faithful to you: and that shall you do, giving the Megalopolitans their city again, and preserving such a number of people as have forsaken it."

Cleomenes pausing awhile, answered [that] it was a hard thing to believe that: "But yet," quoth he, "let honour take place with us, before profit."

After that, he sent a herald straight unto Messena unto them that were fled thither, and told them that he was contented to offer them their city again, so that they would become good friends and confederates of the Lacedaemonians, forsaking the alliance of the Achaeans. [But though Cleomenes made these generous and humane proposals, Philopoemen would not suffer them to break their league with the Achaeans; and accusing Cleomenes to the people, as if his design was not to restore the city, but to take the citizens too, he forced Thearidas and Lysandridas to leave Messene. This news coming to Cleomenes, though he had before taken strict care that the city should not be plundered, yet then, being in anger, and out of all patience, he despoiled the place of all the valuables, and sent the statues and the pictures to Sparta; and demolish[ed] a great part of the city.

Narration and Discussion

Was the plan to capture Megalopolis a good one? Why was it unsuccessful? Where might this leave the Spartans?

Cleomenes said to Lysandrides, "Let honour take place with us, before profit." Dryden translates it, "With us let profit always yield to glory." What did Cleomenes mean?

Lesson Ten

Introduction

In the summer of 222 B.C., the Spartans fought one last time against the combined armies of the Achaean League and the Macedonians. Their defeat was not obvious from the start, although the Spartans were outnumbered (something that didn't usually deter them). If Cleomenes had been able to hold out just a bit longer, Plutarch says, things might have ended differently; but the difference in numbers, a lack of money, and an act of treason combined to spell disaster.

Vocabulary

opprobrious: scornful, critical

garrison: military troops

Phliunta: Dryden: "Philius"

unfoiled: unbeaten

circumspect: cautious, guarded

Historic Occasions

222 B.C.: the Battle of Selasia/Sellasia

Reading

Part One

[Knowing very well that the Macedonians were dispersed into their winter-quarters, and that Antigonus with his friends and a few mercenaries about him wintered in Argos, upon these considerations (Cleomenes) invaded the country of the Argives, hoping to shame Antigonus to a battle upon unequal terms, or else if he did not dare to fight, to disrepute with the Achaeans. And this accordingly happened. For Cleomenes wasting, plundering, and spoiling the whole country, the Argives, in grief and anger at the loss, gathered in crowds at the king's gates, crying out that he should either fight, or surrender his command to better and braver men.]

But Antigonus, like a wise and excellent captain, thinking it a dishonour to him rashly to put himself in danger, and his friends also, though he were provoked with many injuries and **opprobrious** words: would not go into the field, but stood constant in his first determination.

[A little while after, being informed that Antigonus designed a new advance to Tegea, and thence to invade Laconia, (Cleomenes) rapidly took his soldiers, and marching by a side-road, appeared early in the morning before Argos, and wasted the fields about it. The corn he did not cut down, as is usual, with reaping hooks and knives, but beat it down with great wooden staves made like broadswords, as if, in mere contempt and wanton scorn, while travelling on his way, without any effort or trouble, he spoiled and destroyed their harvest.]

But when they came to the [exercise ground] called Cyllabaris, certain of the soldiers going about to have set it afire, Cleomenes would not suffer them, and told them that [the mischief] he had done at Megalopolis was rather angrily than honestly done.

[And when Antigonus, first of all, came hastily back to Argos, and then occupied the mountains and passes with his posts, he professed to disregard and despise it all]; and sent heralds to him to desire the keys of the temple of Juno, [as if] after he had done sacrifice, he would depart his way. Thus mocking Antigonus, after he [Cleomenes] had sacrificed unto the goddess, under the temple that was shut up, he sent his army unto **Phliunta**, and having driven away the **garrison** out of Ologunta, he came unto the city of Orchomenum, having not only encouraged his citizens, but gotten even amongst the enemies themselves a fame also to be a noble captain, and worthy to manage great affairs. For every man judged him to be a skillful soldier, and a valiant captain, that with the power of one only city, [he] did maintain war against the kingdom of Macedon, against all the people of Peloponnesus, and against the treasure of so great a king: and withal, not only to keep his own country of Laconia **unfoiled,** but far otherwise to hurt his enemies' countries, and to take so many great cities of theirs.

Part Two

King Antigonus, who by the greatness of his kingdom did defray the charge of this war, did weary and overcome Cleomenes at the length, because he lacked money both to pay the strangers that served him, and also to maintain his own citizens. For otherwise, doubtless the [advantage of time would have served Cleomenes'] turn well, because the troubles that fell upon Antigonus in his realm, did make him to be sent for home. If these letters had been brought [to] him but a little before the battle, Antigonus [would have] gone his way, and left the Achaeans. But fortune, that always striketh the stroke in all weightiest causes, gave much speed and favour unto time: that immediately after the battle was fought at Selasia (where Cleomenes lost his army and city), the very messengers arrived that came for

Antigonus to come home, the which made the overthrow of King Cleomenes so much more lamentable.

For if he had delayed battle but two days longer, when the Macedonians had been gone, he might have made what peace he would with the Achaeans: but for lack of money, he was driven (as Polybius writeth) to give battle, with twenty thousand men, against thirty thousand: where he shewed himself an excellent and skillful captain, and where his citizens also fought like valiant men, and the strangers in like case did shew themselves good soldiers. But his only overthrow was [first] by the manner of his enemies' weapons, and [second] the force of their battle of footmen.

But Phylarchus writeth, that treason was the cause of his overthrow. For Antigonus had appointed the Acarnanians, and the Illyrians which he had in his army, to steal upon the wings of his enemy's army, where Euclidas, Cleomenes' brother was, to compass him in behind, whilst he did set the rest of his men in battle.

When Cleomenes was got up upon some hill to look about him, to see the countenance of the enemy, and seeing none of the Acarnanians, nor of the Illyrians: he was then afraid of Antigonus, that he went about some stratagem of war. Wherefore he called for Demoteles, whose charge was to take heed of stratagems and secret ambushes, and commanded him to look to the rearward of his army, and to be very **circumspect** all about. Demoteles, that was bribed before (as it is reported) with money, told him that all was clear in the rearward, and bade him look to overthrow his enemies before him. Cleomenes trusting this report, set forward against Antigonus, and in the end, his citizens of Sparta which he had about him, gave such a fierce charge upon the squadron of the Macedonian footmen, that they drave them back [about half a mile] off.

But in the meantime, Euclidas his brother, in the other wing of his army, being compassed in behind, Cleomenes turning him back, and seeing the overthrow, cried out aloud: "Alas, good brother, thou art but slain, yet thou diest valiantly, and honestly, and thy death shall be a worthy example unto all posterity, and shall be sung by the praises of the women of Sparta." So Euclidas and his men being slain, the enemies came straight to set upon Cleomenes' wing. Cleomenes then seeing his men discouraged, and that they durst no longer resist the enemy, fled, and saved himself. Many of the strangers also that served him, were slain at this battle: and of six thousand Spartans, there were left alive but only two hundred.

Part Three

Now Cleomenes being returned unto Sparta, the citizens coming to see him, he gave them counsel to yield themselves unto Antigonus the conqueror: and for himself, if either alive or dead he could do anything for the honour and benefit of Sparta, that he would willingly do it. The women of the city also, coming unto them that fleeing had escaped with him, when he saw them unarm the men, and bring them drink to refresh them with; he also went home to his own house.

Then a maid of the house, which he had taken in the city of Megalopolis (and whom he had entertained ever since the death of his wife) came unto him as her manner was, to refresh him coming hot from the battle: howbeit he would not drink though he was extreme dry, nor sit being very weary, but armed as he was, laid his arm across upon a pillar, and leaning his head upon it, reposed himself a little, and casting in his mind all the ways that were to be thought of; [and then with his friends set out at once for] the haven of Gythium, and there having his ships which he had appointed for the purpose, he hoisted sail, and departed his way.

Immediately after his departure, came Antigonus into the city of Sparta, and courteously entreated the citizens and inhabitants he found, and did offend no man, nor proudly despise the ancient honour and dignity of Sparta but referring them to their own laws and government. When he had sacrificed to the gods for his victory, he departed from thence the third day, news being brought him that the war was very great in Macedon, and that the barbarous people did spoil his country.

[Antigonus died shortly after this.]

Narration and Discussion

Plutarch says that Cleomenes had ships ready to sail him away in the harbour. Had he perhaps foreseen a possible loss in this battle?

Antigonus appears to have been an unexpectedly gracious victor over the Spartans. As a creative narration, cover these events as a Spartan news reporter (or a news team, if you have a group). You may want to interview Spartan citizens, or Antigonus himself.

Lesson Eleven

Introduction

After losing his kingdom at the Battle of Selasia, Cleomenes escaped to Egypt, where he hoped to find protection, and possibly some support for the Spartan cause.

Vocabulary

vaunt: boast

no special good: no great welcome

lasciviousness: depravity, sinfulness

tabor: drum

privy council: private advisors

strangers: foreigners

Reading

Part One

Now Cleomenes departing out the Isle of Cythera, went and cast anchor in another island, called Aegialia. Then determining to sail over to the city of Cyrena, Therycion, one of Cleomenes' friends (a man that in wars shewed himself very valiant, but a boaster beside of his own doings) took Cleomenes aside, and said thus unto him:

> "Truly O King, we have lost an honourable occasion
> to die in battle, though every man hath heard us
> **vaunt** and say, that Antigonus should never
> overcome the king of Sparta alive, but dead. A
> second occasion yet is offered us to die, with much
> less honour and fame notwithstanding, than the

first. Whither do we sail to no purpose? Why do we
flee the death at hand, and seek it so far off? If it be
no shame nor dishonour for the posterity and race
of Hercules to serve the successors of Philip and
Alexander: let us save ourselves unto Antigonus,
who in likelihood will better use us than Ptolemy,
because the Macedonians are far more nobler
persons than the Egyptians. And if we disdain to be
commanded by them which have overcome us in
battle, why then will we make him lord of us, that
hath not overcome us: instead of one, to make us
inferior unto both, fleeing Antigonus, and serving
King Ptolemy? Can we say that we go into Egypt, in
respect to see your mother there? A joyful sight no
doubt, when she shall shew King Ptolemy's wives
her son, that before was a king, a prisoner, and
fugitive now. Were it not better for us, that having
yet Laconia our country in sight, and our swords
besides in our own hands, to deliver us from this
great misery, [and clear ourselves to those who at
Selasia died for the honour and defense of Sparta?
Or, shall we sit lazily in Egypt, inquiring what news
from Sparta, and whom Antigonus hath been
pleased to make governor of Lacedaemon]?"

Therycion ending his oration, Cleomenes answered him thus:

"Dost thou think it a glory for thee to seek death,
which is the easiest matter, and the presentest unto
any man, that can be and yet, wretch that thou art,
thou fleest now more cowardly and shamefully,
than from the battle. For divers valiant men, and far
better than ourselves, have often yielded unto their
enemies, either by some misfortune, or compelled
by greater number and multitude of men: but he,
say I, that submitteth himself unto pain and misery
[because of the] reproach and praise of men, he
cannot but confess that he is overcome by his own
unhappiness. For, when a man will willingly kill
himself, he must not do it to be rid of pains and
labour, but it must have an honourable respect and
action. For, to live or die for his own respect, that

cannot but be dishonourable: the which now thou persuadest me unto, to make me flee this present misery we are in, without any honour or profit in our death. And therefore, I am of opinion, that we should not yet cast off the hope we have to serve our country in time to come: but when all hope faileth us, then we may easily make ourselves away when we list."

Thereunto Therycion gave no answer, but as soon as he found opportunity to slip from Cleomenes, he went to the seaside, and slew himself.

Part Two

Cleomenes hoisting sail from the Isle of Aegialia, [landed in Libya], and was brought by the king's servants unto the city of Alexandria. King Ptolemy at his first coming, gave Cleomenes **no special good**, but indifferent entertainment. But after that he had shewed himself to be of great wisdom and judgment, and that Ptolemy saw in the simplicity of his Laconian life he had also a noble disposition and courage, nothing [unbecoming his birth], and that he yielded not to his adversity: he took more delight in his company, than in all the company of his flatterers and hangers on him. He then repented him greatly, that he had made no more account of him before, but had suffered him to be overthrown by Antigonus, who through the victory [over the Spartans], had marvellously enlarged his honour and power. Then he began to comfort Cleomenes, and doing him as great honour as could be, promised that he would send him with ships and money into Greece, and put him again into his kingdom: and further, gave him an annual pension in the meantime, of four-and-twenty talents, with the which he simply and soberly entertained himself and his men about him: and bestowed all the rest [in assisting] his countrymen that came out of Greece into Egypt.

Part Three

But now, old King Ptolemy [dying] before he could perform the promise he made unto Cleomenes, to send him into Greece: the realm falling then into great **lasciviousness**, drunkenness, and into the government of women, his case and misery was clean forgotten. For the young king his son was so given over to women and wine, that when he was most sober, and in his best wits, he most disposed himself to make feasts and sacrifices, and to have the **tabor** playing in his court, to gather people together, like a stage player or juggler, whilst [his women] did rule all the affairs of the state.

But when he [Ptolemy IV] came to be king, it appeared he had need of Cleomenes: because he was afraid of his brother Magas, who by his mother's means, was very well esteemed of among soldiers. Wherefore he called Cleomenes to him, and made him [one] of his **privy council**, [and acquainted him with the design of taking off his brother]. All other [of] his friends did counsel him to do it: but Cleomenes only vehemently dissuaded him from it, and told him, that if it were possible, rather more brethren should be begotten unto the king for the safety of his person, and for dividing of the affairs of the kingdom between them.

Amongst the king's familiars that was chiefest about him, there was one Sosibius, that said unto Cleomenes: so long as [Ptolemy's] brother Magas lived, the soldiers that be strangers, whom the king entertained, would never be true to him. Cleomenes answered him, [that] for that matter there was no danger: for saith he, of those hired strangers, there are three thousand Peloponnesians, which he knew at the twinkling of an eye, would be at his commandment, to come with their armour and weapon[s] where he would appoint them.

These words of Cleomenes at that time shewed his faith and good will he bare unto the king, and the force he was of besides. But afterwards, Ptolemy's fearfulness increasing his mistrust: (as it commonly happeneth, that they that lack wit, think it the best safety to be fearful of every wagging of a straw, and to mistrust every man) the remembrance of Cleomenes' words made him much suspected of the courtiers, understanding that he could do so much with the soldiers that were **strangers**: insomuch as some of them said, "See (meaning Cleomenes), there is a lion amongst sheep." Indeed, considering his fashions and behaviour, they might well say so of him: for he would look through his fingers as though he saw nothing, and yet saw all what they did.

Narration and Discussion

Why did Therycion think it would be better to face Antigonus, rather than flee to Egypt? What was Cleomenes' response?

How were Cleomenes' words to Sosibius misinterpreted? Are there any lessons to be learned from this?

Lesson Twelve

Introduction

Cleomenes expected that his safety in Egypt would continue, but he soon became the victim of a conspiracy. By the time he realized his own danger, escape seemed unlikely.

Vocabulary

required: requested

masques: parties

keep his house: he was placed under house arrest

timbrel: tambourine

fair and softly: slowly

repulsed, and put by his purpose: stymied in his attempts

yielded up the ghost: died

People

Ptolemy the son of Chrysermus: there are three Ptolemys in this passage

Antigonus, a brave warrior, and a man of action: an interesting contrast to the negative terms used in **Lesson Seven**

Historic Occasions

219 B.C.: the death of Cleomenes

Reading

Part One

[Cleomenes] **required** an army and ships of the king: and understanding also that Antigonus was dead, and that the Achaeans and Aetolians were at great wars together, and that the affairs of his country did call him home, all Peloponnesus being in arms and uproar, he prayed that they would licence him to depart with his friends. But never a man would give ear unto him, and the king also heard nothing of it, because he was continually entertained among ladies, with banquets, dancing, and **masques**.

But Sosibius, that ruled all the realm, thought that to keep Cleomenes against his will, were a hard thing, and also dangerous: and to let him go also, knowing that he was a valiant man, and of a stirring mind, and one that knew the vices and imperfections of their government: he thought that also no safe way, since no gifts nor presents that could be offered him, could soften him.

Now Cleomenes standing in these terms, there arrived in Alexandria one Nicagoras Messenian, who maliced Cleomenes in his heart, but yet shewed as though he loved him. This Nicagoras on a time had sold Cleomenes certain land, but was not paid for it, either because he had no present money, or else by occasion of the wars which gave him no leisure to make payment. Cleomenes, one day by chance walking upon the sands, he saw Nicagoras landing out of his ship, being newly arrived, and knowing him, he courteously welcomed him, and asked what wind had brought him into Egypt. Nicagoras gently saluting him again, told him that he had brought the king excellent horse[s] of service. Cleomenes smiling, told him, "Thou hadst been better have brought him some [dancers and people to amuse him, *my paraphrase*], for they would have pleased the king better." Nicagoras faintly laughed at his answer, but within [a] few days after he did put him in remembrance of the land he sold him, and prayed him then that he would help him to money, telling him that he would not have pressed him for it, but that he had sustained loss by merchandise.

Cleomenes answered him, that all his pension was spent [that] he had of the king. Nicagoras being offended with this answer, he went and told Sosibius of the mock Cleomenes gave the king. Sosibius was glad of this occasion, but yet desiring further matter to make the king offended with Cleomenes, he persuaded Nicagoras to write a letter to the king against Cleomenes, as though he had conspired to take the city of Cyrena, if the king had given him ships, money, and men of war. When Nicagoras had written this letter, he took ship, and hoisted sail.

Four days after his departure, Sosibius brought his letter to the king, as though he had but newly received it. The king upon sight of it was so offended with Cleomenes, that he gave present order he should be shut up in a great house, where he should have his ordinary diet allowed him, howbeit that he should **keep his house**.

Part Two

This grieved Cleomenes much, but yet he was worse afraid of that which was to come, by this occasion: **Ptolemy the son of Chrysermus**, one of the king's familiars, who had oftentimes before been very conversant and familiar with Cleomenes, and did frankly talk together in all matters: Cleomenes one day sent for him, to pray him to come unto him. Ptolemy came at his request, and familiarly discoursing together, went about to dissuade him from all the suspicions he had, and excused the king also for that he had done unto him: so taking his leave he left him, not thinking that Cleomenes followed him (as he did) to the gate, where he sharply took up the soldiers, saying, that they were very negligent and careless in looking to "such a fearful beast as he was," and so ill to be taken, if he once [e]scaped their hands. Cleomenes heard what he said, and went into his lodging again, Ptolemy knowing nothing that he was behind him: and [Cleomenes] reported the very words again unto his friends.

Then all the Spartans converting their good hope into anger, determined to be revenged of the injury Ptolemy had done them, and to die like noble Spartans, [and not stay till, like fatted sacrifices, they were butchered. For it was both grievous and dishonourable for Cleomenes, who had scorned to come to terms with **Antigonus, a brave warrior, and a man of action**, to wait an effeminate king's leisure, till he should lay aside his **timbrel** and end his dance, and then kill him]. They being fully resolved hereof, as you have heard: King Ptolemy by chance went unto the city of Canobus [*or Canopus*], and first they gave out in Alexandria, that the king minded to set Cleomenes at liberty. Then Cleomenes' friends observing the custom of the kings of Egypt, when they meant to set a prisoner at liberty (which was, to send the prisoners meat, and presents) did sent unto him such manner of presents, and so deceived the soldiers that had the keeping of him, saying, that they brought those presents from the king. For Cleomenes himself did sacrifice unto the gods, and sent unto the soldiers that kept him, part of those presents that were sent unto him, and supping with his friends that night, made merry with them, every man being crowned with garlands.

Part Three

Cleomenes about noon, perceiving the soldiers had taken in their cups, and that they were asleep: he put on his coat, and [ripping it open] on the right shoulder, went out of the house with his sword drawn in his hand, accompanied with his friends, following him in that sort, which were thirty in all.

Amongst them there was one called Hippotas, who being lame, went very lively out with them at the first: but when he saw they went **fair and softly** because of him, he prayed them to kill him, because they should not hinder their enterprise for a lame man that could do them no service. Notwithstanding, by chance they met with a townsman a-horseback, that came hard by their door, whom they plucked from his horse, and cast Hippotas upon him: and then ran through the city, and cried to the people, "Liberty, liberty."

Now the people had no other courage in them, but only commended Cleomenes, and wondered at his valiantness: but otherwise to follow him, or to further his enterprise, not a man of them had any heart in them. Thus running up and down the town, they met with Ptolemy (the same whom we said before was the son of Chrysermus) as he came out of the court: whereupon three of them setting on him, slew him presently. There was also another Ptolemy that was governor and lieutenant of the city of Alexandria: who hearing a rumour of this stir, came unto him in his coach. They went and met him, and first having driven away his guard and soldiers that went before him, they plucked him out of his coach, and slew him also. After that they went towards the castle, with intent to set all the prisoners there at liberty to take their part. Howbeit the jailers that kept them had so strongly locked up the prison doors, that Cleomenes was **repulsed, and put by his purpose**. Thus wandering up and down the city, no man neither came to join with him, nor to resist him, for every man fled for fear of him. Wherefore at length being weary with going up and down, he turned him to his friends, and said unto them: "It is no marvel [that] women command such a cowardly people, that flee in this sort from their liberty." Thereupon he prayed them all to die like men, and like those that were brought up with him, and that were worthy of the fame of his so noble deeds.

Then the first man that made himself be slain, was Hippotas, who died of a wound one of the young men of his company gave him with a sword at his request. After him every man slew themselves, one after another, without any fear at all, saving Panteas, who was the first man that entered the city of Megalopolis. He was a fair young man, and had been very well brought up in the Laconian discipline, and better than any man of his years. Cleomenes did love him dearly, and commanded him that when he should see he were dead, and all the rest also, that then he should kill himself last of all.

Now they all being laid on the ground, he [Panteas] searched them one after another with the point of his sword, to see if there were any of them yet let alive: and when he had pricked Cleomenes on the heel amongst others, and saw that he did yet knit his brows, he kissed him, and sat down by him. Then perceiving that he had **yielded up the ghost**, embracing him when he was dead, he also slew himself, and fell upon him. Thus Cleomenes having reigned [as] king of Sparta sixteen years, being the same manner of man we have described him to be: he ended his days in this sort as ye hear.

Narration and Discussion

What outcome did Cleomenes and his companions expect from their attempted rebellion? What seems to have finally discouraged them and caused them to take their own lives?

What are some characteristics of heroes? Would you call either Agis or Cleomenes a hero?

For older students, or those wishing to go deeper:

Plutarch's original introduction to *Agis and Cleomenes* contains these lines:

> Overmuch praise is dangerous in every person, but chiefly in ambitious governors. For if they be men of great power, it makes them commit many desperate parts [acts]: for they will not allow that honour proceeds of virtue, but that honour is virtue itself...

> For they... seeking to increase the power of the common people, and to restore the just and honest government again of the commonwealth of Lacedaemon, which for long time had been out of use: did in like manner purchase the hate of the nobility, which were loath to lose any part of their wonted covetousness.

Continue the passage, in the style of Plutarch, describing the lives and leadership of Agis and Cleomenes.

The Plutarch Project

Tiberius and Gaius Gracchus

(Second Century B.C.)

The World of the Gracchi

The Gracchi brothers, Tiberius and Gaius, were born in a time of political, economic, and social upheaval in Rome, not unlike the later Industrial Revolution in Europe. During recent wars, much of Italy's farmland had been devastated. Men from rural areas were conscripted for faraway military service, and many of them never returned. The family members left were no longer able to maintain even their small farms, and they moved in large numbers to the cities, particularly Rome, hoping to make some kind of living there. With many newly wealthy and lazy urbanites as potential employers or customers, finding success in the city wasn't an impossible idea; but as so many people flooded in, not everyone did well, and living conditions were often wretched. Another disadvantage of this trend (at least for Rome) was that non-land-owners were disqualified for army service.

Ignoring the law that restricted any private landowner to 500 *iugera* (a *iugerum* was equal to 0.623 acres or 0.25 hectares), sharp Roman businessmen bought out or out-rented the struggling farmers (see **Lesson Three**), and consolidated the small plots of land into big commercial operations, with slaves doing most of the work. (There were more slaves than ever now because of Roman military victories, and although this had its benefits, there was a real fear that one day the slaves would revolt.) Some of the land being bought up was *ager publicus*, or common land, which was never intended to be held privately. A lot of money was also changing hands through government contracts; a number of people were becoming very wealthy by supplying the army with weapons or tents, by running construction companies or mines, and by collecting certain types of taxes and rents that came with those contracts. You may recognize the term "publican" from the Bible, and that was the name for these contractors: *publicani*. Plutarch refers to them as simply the "wealthy men," those who were more interested in protecting their contracts and their money than in social justice.

How important were tribunes?

The responsibility of a non-military tribune (tribune of the plebeians, or plebs) was to protect the liberties of the people from any individual or group (such as the nobles) who might take advantage of them or suppress their rights; for example by creating unjust laws. This position was not part of the junior-senior ranking of magistrates such as quaestor and consul; it was an office voted on by the common people (plebeians), who were bound by oath to protect the tribunes from harm. (There would be more than one tribune in office at a time, usually ten.) Ex-consuls could but did not usually become tribunes; one exception was Marcus Fulvius Flaccus, a supporter of the Gracchi.

This view of tribunes as "sancrosanct," too holy to be interfered with (even by each other), was a large part of the story of the Gracchi.

What was the *Lex Sempronia Agraria*?

This was the proposal for land reform that Tiberius Gracchus made in 133 B.C., which is explained in detail in this *Life*. It is also called the *Lex Agraria* or Law Agraria.

Names that are easy to confuse

Gracchi or Gracchus?

Thomas North titled the whole *Life* "Tiberius and Caius Gracchi." Dryden's translation separated the two and called them "Tiberius Gracchus" and "Gaius Gracchus." Gracchus is the singular, and Gracchi is the plural.

Caius or Gaius?

North spelled it Caius Gracchus, the same way that he spelled Caius Marius and Caius Julius Caesar. By the time of Dryden's translation, the common English spelling of this name was Gaius, and that is what I have used.

Two Tiberiuses

Tiberius Gracchus was named for his father, who was "twice consul and once censor," and who married Cornelia, the daughter of Scipio Africanus the Elder (see below).

Two Scipios

Scipio Africanus the Elder was a Roman general, who fought with Hannibal in the Punic Wars; he was the grandfather of Tiberius and Gaius.

The younger Scipio Africanus was his adopted grandson Publius Cornelius Scipio Aemilianus Africanus Numantinus (185–129 BC), or Scipio Africanus the Younger. Plutarch called him the man "whom the people of Rome ... had loved better than any man else whatsoever." He is mentioned several times, including his reaction to the death of Tiberius (in **Lesson Seven**), and a note about his own death (in **Lesson Ten**). This Scipio married the sister of the Gracchi.

Lesson One

Introduction

Two brothers; sons of a consul and censor; grandsons of the famous Scipio Africanus the Elder. Yet the biggest influence on their young lives seemed to be their mother, Cornelia, who raised and educated them with a goal of greatness. You may remember reading "Cornelia's Jewels" in *Fifty Famous Stories Retold*.

Vocabulary

Castor and Pollux: the mythological twins in the constellation Gemini

jetted: blew up and down

pulpit, pulpit for orations: the Rostra, or speakers' platform

orators: public speakers (see introduction to *Julius Caesar*)

full of fineness and curiosity: Dryden, "vehement and rich," meaning rich in detail

curiously and superfluously: Dryden, he had "a fondness for new fashions and rarities"

dolphins of silver: something for the mantelpiece, maybe?

an instrument of music: Dryden, "a sort of pitchpipe"

the justice unto their tenants: Dryden translates this "their justice in the government of its subjects"

continency against voluptuousness: self-control regarding pleasure

fell out at sundry times: took place in different time periods

peradventure: perhaps

People

Scipio (the Elder) and **the younger Scipio Africanus:** see introductory note

Historic Occasions

169-163 B.C. (uncertain): birth of Tiberius Gracchus

154 B.C.: birth of Gaius Gracchus (Plutarch says that they were born nine years apart); and the death of Tiberius Gracchus Senior

Reading

Now that we have declared unto you the history of the lives of these two Grecians, Agis and Cleomenes aforesaid: we must also write the history of two Romans, the which is no less lamentable for the troubles and calamities that chanced unto Tiberius and Gaius, both of them the sons of Tiberius Gracchus.

He, having been twice consul, and once censor, and having had the honour of two triumphs, had notwithstanding more honour and fame only for his valiantness, for the which he was thought worthy to marry with Cornelia, the daughter of **Scipio [Africanus the Elder]** who overcame Hannibal, after [Scipio's] death: though while he lived he was never his friend, but rather his enemy.

It is reported that Tiberius, on a time, found two snakes in his bed, and that the soothsayers and wizards having considered the signification thereof, did forbid him to kill them both, and also to let them both escape; but one only: assuring him that if he killed the male, he should not live long after: and if he killed the female, that then his wife Cornelia should die. Tiberius then loving his wife dearly, thinking it meeter for him also, that he being the elder of both, and she yet a young woman, should die before her: he slew the male, and let the female escape, howbeit he died soon after, leaving twelve children alive, all of them begotten of Cornelia.

Cornelia after the death of her husband, taking upon her the rule of her house and children, led such a chaste life, was so good to her children, and of so noble a mind, [that Tiberius seemed to all men to have done nothing unreasonable in choosing to die for such a woman]. She remaining [a] widow, King Ptolemy made suit unto her, and would have made her his wife and queen. But she refused, and in her widowhood lost all her children, but one daughter (whom she bestowed upon **the younger Scipio Africanus**), and Tiberius and Gaius, whose lives we presently write.

Those she so carefully brought up, that they [became] more civil, and better conditioned, than any other Romans in their time; every man judged, that education prevailed more in them than nature. For, as in the [statues] and pictures of **Castor and Pollux**, there is a certain difference discerned, whereby a man may know that the one was made for wrestling, and the other for running: even so between these two young brethren, amongst other [things] the great likeness between them, being both happily born to be valiant, to be temperate, to be liberal, to be learned, and to be nobly minded. There grew, notwithstanding, great difference in their actions and doings in the commonwealth: the which I think convenient to declare, before I proceed any farther.

First of all, for the favour of the face, the look and moving of the body, Tiberius was much more mild and tractable, and Gaius more hot and earnest. For the first in his orations was very modest, and kept his place and the other of all the Romans was the first, that in his oration **jetted** up and down the **pulpit**, and that plucked his gown over his shoulders: as they write of Cleon [the] Athenian, that he was the first of all **orators** that opened his gown, and clapped his hand on his thigh in his oration. Furthermore, Gaius' words, and the vehemency of his persuasion, were terrible [*Dryden: impetuous*] and full of passion: but Tiberius' words in contrary manner, were mild, and moved men more to compassion, being very proper, and excellently applied, where Gaius' words were **full of fineness and curiosity**.

The like difference also was between them in their fare and diet. For Tiberius [was frugal and plain]: and Gaius also, in respect of other Romans, lived very temperately; but in respect of his brother's fare, **curiously and superfluously**. Insomuch as Drusus [once] reproved him, because he had bought certain **dolphins of silver**, to the value of a thousand two hundred and fifty drachmas for every pound weight.

And now, as touching the manners and natural disposition of them both, agreeing with the diversity of their tongues, [Tiberius] being mild and plausible; and [Gaius] hot and choleric, insomuch that other-while, forgetting himself in his oration, against his will he would be very earnest, and strain his voice beyond his compass, and so with great uncomeliness confound his words. Yet finding his own fault, he devised this remedy. He had a servant called Licinius, a good wise man, who with **an instrument of music** he had, by the which they teach men to rise and fall in their tunes. When [Gaius] was in his oration, [Licinius] ever stood behind him: and when he perceived that his master's voice was a little too loud, and that through choler he exceeded his ordinary speech: he played a soft [note] behind him, at the sound whereof Gaius immediately fell from his extremity, and easily came to himself again. And here was the diversity between them. Otherwise, for their hardiness against their enemies, **the justice unto their tenants**, the care and pains in their offices of charge, and also their **continency against voluptuousness**: in all these they were both alike.

For age, Tiberius was elder by nine years, by reason whereof their several authority and doings in the commonwealth **fell out at sundry times**. And this was one of the chiefest causes why their doings prospered not, because they had not both authority in one self time, neither could they join their power together: the which if it had met at one self time, had been of great force, and **peradventure** invincible. Wherefore we must write particularly of them both, but first of all we must begin with the elder.

He, when he came to man's [e]state, had such a name and estimation, that immediately they made him fellow in the college of the priests, which at Rome are called *augurs*: (being those that have the charge to consider of signs and predictions of things to come), more for his valiantness than for nobility. The same doth Appius Claudius witness unto us, one that hath been both consul and censor, and also president of the Senate, and of greater authority than any man in his time. This Appius at a supper when all the augurs were together, after he had saluted Tiberius, and made very much of him, he offered him his daughter in marriage. Tiberius was very glad of the offer, and therewithal the [agreement of] marriage was presently concluded between them. Thereupon Appius coming home to his house, at the threshold of his door he called aloud for his wife, and told her: "Antistia, I have bestowed our daughter Claudia." She, wondering at it, "O gods," said she, "and what needed all this haste? What couldst thou have done more, if thou hadst gotten her Tiberius Gracchus for her husband?"

Narration and Discussion

Creative narration: create a "wanted" or similar poster, showing the two brothers and how to tell them apart. (You may find it useful to keep this and add extra notes as you work through this *Life*.)

Plutarch says that the great likeness between the brothers is that they were both "happily born to be valiant, to be temperate, to be liberal, to be learned, and to be nobly minded." But he also commends their mother, because she so "carefully brought [them] up, that they [became] more civil, and better conditioned, than any other Romans in their time; every man judged, that education prevailed more in them than nature." Can both be true?

Lesson Two

Introduction

In this lesson we focus on the early career of Tiberius, the elder brother. He began, like many young Roman men, as a soldier in Africa (serving under his brother-in-law Scipio). After winning his first position in civil government, he was sent out to deal with a crisis situation in what is now Spain: a war with the Numantines that had been dragging on for twenty years, and that was about to get worse.

Vocabulary

indued: endowed, gifted

treasurer: Dryden translates this "paymaster," but it means the office of quaestor

empire of Rome: this was during the time of the Republic, so it is a general term only

preferred: proposed

Historic Occasions

137 B.C.: Tiberius became quaestor and went to Numantia

Reading

Now Tiberius (the younger) being in the wars in Africa under Scipio the second, who had married his sister: he found his captain **indued** with many noble gifts of nature, to allure men's hearts to desire to follow his valiantness. So in a short time he [Tiberius] did excel all the young men of his time, as well in obedience, as in the valiantness of his person: insomuch that he was the first man that scaled the walls of the enemies, as Fannius reporteth, who sayeth that he scaled the walls with him, and did help him in that valiant enterprise. So that being present, all the camp were in love with him: and when he was absent, every man wished for him again.

After this war was ended, he was chosen **treasurer**, and it was his chance to go against the Numantines, with Gaius Mancinus, one of the consuls, who was an honest man, but yet had the worst luck of any captain the Romans had. Notwithstanding, Tiberius' wisdom and valiantness, in this extreme ill luck of his captain, did not only appear with great glory to him, but also most wonderful, the great obedience and reverence he bare unto his captain: though his misfortunes did so trouble and grieve him, that he could not tell himself, whether he was captain or not.

For when he was overthrown in [various great battles, he endeavoured to dislodge by night and leave his camp]. The Numantines hearing of it, first took his camp, and then ran after them that fled, and setting upon the rearward, slew them, and environed all his army. So that they were driven into strait and narrow places, where out they could by no means escape.

Thereupon Mancinus, despairing that he could get out by force, sent a herald to the enemies to treat of peace. The Numantines made answer, that they would trust no man but Tiberius only, and therefore they willed he should be sent unto them. They desired that, partly for the love they bare unto the virtues of the young man, because there was no talk of any other in all this war but of him: and partly also, as remembering his father Tiberius, who making wars in Spain, and having there subdued many nations, [had] granted the Numantines peace, the which he caused the Romans afterwards to confirm and ratify.

Hereupon Tiberius was sent to speak with them, and partly obtaining that [which] he desired, and partly also granting them that [which] they required: he concluded peace with them, whereby assuredly he saved the lives of twenty thousand Roman citizens, besides slaves and other stragglers that willingly followed the camp.

This notwithstanding, the Numantines took the spoil of all the goods they found in the Romans' camp, among the which they found Tiberius' books of account, touching the money disbursed of the treasure in his charge. Tiberius being marvellous desirous to have his books again, returned back to Numantia with two or three of his friends only, though the army of the Romans were gone far on their way. So coming to the town, he spake unto the governors of the city, and prayed them to redeliver him his books of account, because his malicious enemies should not accuse him, calling him to account for his doings. The Numantines were very glad of this good hap, and prayed them to come into the town. He standing still in doubt with himself what to do, whether he should go into the town or not: the governors of the city came to him, and taking him by the hand, prayed he would think they were not his enemies, but good friends, and that he would trust them.

Whereupon Tiberius thought best to yield to their persuasion, being desirous also to have his books again, and the rather, for fear of offending the Numantines, if he should have denied and mistrusted them. When he was brought into the city, they provided his dinner, and were very earnest with him, entreating him to dine with them. Then they gave him his books again, and offered him moreover to take what he would of all the spoils they had gotten in the camp of the Romans. Howbeit of all that he would take nothing but frankincense, which he used when he did any sacrifice for his country: and then taking his leave of them, with thanks he returned.

When he was returned to Rome, all this peace concluded was utterly misliked, as dishonourable to the majesty of the **empire of Rome**. Yet the parents and friends of them that had served in this war, making the greatest part of the people: they gathered about Tiberius, saying that what faults were committed in this service, they were to impute it unto the consul Mancinus, and not unto Tiberius, who had saved such a number of Romans' lives. For they gave order, that the consul Mancinus should be sent naked and bound unto the Numantines, and for Tiberius' sake, they pardoned all the rest.

I think Scipio [*Africanus the Younger*], who bare great sway at that time in Rome, and was a man of greatest account, did help [Tiberius]

140

at that pinch: who, notwithstanding, was ill thought of, because he [Scipio] did not also save the consul Mancinus, and confirm the peace concluded with the Numantines, considering it was made by Tiberius, his friend and kinsman. But these mislikings grew chiefly through the ambition of Tiberius' friends, and certain learned men, which stirred him up against Scipio. But yet it fell not out to open malice between them, neither followed there any hurt upon it. And surely I am persuaded, that Tiberius [would not have] fallen into those troubles he did afterwards, if Scipio Africanus had been present, when he passed those things he **preferred**. But Scipio was then in wars at the [*final*] Siege of Numantia.

Narration and Discussion

The Numantines insisted that they would trust or deal with Tiberius, and Tiberius only. What were their reasons?

When Tiberius realized that his account books were missing, what were his options? What would you have done?

Why was the peace treaty "misliked?" Does that give any hint that Tiberius might have a harder time gaining respect at home, than he did with the Numantines?

Lesson Three

Introduction

The next four lessons all take place in the pivotal year of 133 B.C. Tiberius, having both travelled and gained knowledge of economics, wanted to do something about the problems he had seen inside and outside of Rome. His responsibility as tribune was to promote the rights of the common people; but his vision for reform clashed with other private interests.

Vocabulary

over their heads: into their possession

nor cared any more: they were not so careful about the education of their children

left Italy: moved away, at least from the farming areas; many families went to try to make a living in Rome

desisted: ceased

tribune: see introductory note

who did twit her sons in the teeth: she scolded or teased them

Scipio's mother-in-law: Dryden translates this "the daughter of Scipio," but both are true (see introductory note).

the high Bishop: *Pontifex Maximus*; see note for *Julius Caesar*

avarice: greed

Law Agraria: *Lex Sempronia Agraria*; see introductory note

confute: contradict

People

Mucius Scaevola the lawyer, that then was consul: Publius **Mucius** Scaevola was one of the consuls in 133 B.C., and *Pontifex Maximus* in 131 B.C. His brother Publius Licinius **Crassus** Dives Mucianus was *Pontifex Maximus* in 132 B.C., consul in 131 B.C., and died in 130 B.C. He (**Crassus the high Bishop**, or *Pontifex Maximus*) was also the father-in-law of Gaius Gracchus; his daughter was called Licinia Crassi.

Historic Occasions

133 B.C.: Tiberius was elected tribune and proposed land reforms; Scipio Africanus ended the war in Numantia

Reading

Part One: a little history

When the Romans in old time had overcome any of their neighbours, for ransom they took oftentimes a great deal of their land from them, part whereof they sold [publicly], for the benefit of the commonwealth, and part also they reserved to their state as [common land], which afterwards was let out to farm for a small rent yearly, to the poor citizens that had no lands. Howbeit the rich men [began to offer larger rents], and so began to thrust out the poor men. Thereupon was an ordinance made, that no citizen of Rome should have above five hundred *iugera* [of] land. This law for a time did bridle the covetousness of the rich men, and did ease the poor also that dwelt in the country, upon the farms they had taken up of the commonwealth, and so lived with their own, or with that their ancestors had from the beginning.

But by process of time, their rich neighbours, by names of other men, got their farms **over their heads**, and in the end, the most of them were openly seen in it in their own names. Whereupon, the poor people being thus turned out of all, went but with faint courage afterwards to the war, **nor cared any more for bringing up of children**: so that in short time, the free men **left Italy**, and slaves and barbarous people did replenish it, whom the rich men made to plough those lands which they had taken from the Romans. Gaius Laelius, one of Scipio's friends, gave an attempt to reform this abuse: but because the chiefest of the city were against him, fearing it would break out to some uproar, he **desisted** from his purpose, and therefore he was called Laelius the Wise.

Part Two: the time of Tiberius

But Tiberius being chosen **tribune**, he did forthwith prefer the reformation aforesaid, being allured unto it (as divers writers report) by Diophanes the **orator**, and Blossius the philosopher: of the which, Diophanes was [a refugee] from the city of Mitylene, and Blossius, [an] Italian from the city of Cuma, who was [a student of] Antipater of Tarsus, by whom he was honoured by certain works of philosophy he dedicated unto him. And some also do accuse their mother

Cornelia, **who did twit her sons in the teeth**, that the Romans did yet call her **Scipio's mother-in-law**, and not the mother of the Gracchi. Other[s] say [*the influence on him*] was Spurius Postumius, a companion of Tiberius, and one that contended with him in eloquence. For Tiberius returning from the wars, and finding him far beyond him in fame and reputation, and well-beloved of everyone: he sought to excel him by attempting this noble enterprise, and of so great expectation.

His own brother Gaius, in a certain book, wrote that as he [*Tiberius*] went to the wars of Numantia, passing through Tuscany, he found the country in manner unhabited: and they that did follow the plough, or keep beasts, were the most of them slaves, and barbarous people, come out of a strange country. Whereupon ever after it ran in his mind to bring this enterprise to pass, which brought great troubles to their house. But in fine, it was the people only that most set his heart afire to covet honour, and that hastened his determination: first bringing him to it by bills set up on every wall, in every porch, and upon the tombs, praying him by them to cause the poor citizens of Rome to have their lands restored, which were belonging to the commonwealth.

This notwithstanding he himself made not the law alone of his own head, but did it by the counsel and advice of the chiefest men of Rome, for virtue and estimation: among the which, **Crassus the high Bishop** was one, and **Mucius Scaevola the lawyer, that then was consul**, and Appius Claudius, his father-in-law. And truly it seemeth, that never [a] law was made with greater favour, than that which he preferred against so great injustice, and avarice. For those that should have been punished for transgressing the law, and should have had the lands taken from them by force, which they unjustly kept against the law of Rome, [were notwithstanding to receive a price for quitting their unlawful claims, and giving up their lands to those fit owners who stood in need of help.].

Now though the reformation established by this law was done with such great favour: the people notwithstanding were contented, and [*were willing to*] forget all that was past, so that they might have no more wrong offered them in time to come. But the rich men, and men of great possessions, hated the law for their **avarice**, and for spite and self-will (which would not let them yield) they were at deadly feud with the lawyer that had preferred the law, and [they] sought by all device they could to dissuade the people from it: telling them that Tiberius brought in this **Law Agraria** again, to disturb the commonwealth, and to make some alteration in the state.

But they prevailed not. For Tiberius defending the matter, which of itself was good and just, with such eloquence as might have justified [even] an evil cause, was invincible: and no man was able to argue against him to **confute** him, when speaking in the behalf of the poor citizens of Rome. The people being gathered round about the pulpit for orations, he told them that the wild beasts through Italy had their dens and caves of abode, and that the men that fought, and were slain for their country, had nothing else but air and light, and so were compelled to wander up and down with their wives and children, having no resting place nor house to put their heads in: and that the captains do but mock their soldiers, when they encourage them in battle to fight valiantly for the graves, the temples, their own houses, and their predecessors. "For," said he, "of such a number of poor citizens as there be, there cannot a man of them shew any ancient house or tomb of their ancestors: because the poor men do go to the wars, and be slain for the rich men's pleasures and wealth: besides they falsely call them lords of the earth, where they have not a handful of ground that is theirs."

These and such other like words being uttered before all the people with such vehemency and truth, did so move the common people withal, and put them in such a rage, that there was no adversary of his able to withstand him.

Narration and Discussion

Why was the name "Laelius the Wise" ironic?

How did Tiberius' army travels open his eyes to the needs of those living in rural areas of Italy? What were the other influences on his movement for land reform?

For older students: The Senate had become extremely powerful; this was partly because of the Romans' recent need for military leadership (during the Punic Wars). The time was now ripe for more democracy in Rome, and perhaps if the Gracchi brothers had not come forward, someone else would have sparked a similar move to reform. But in a later lesson, Gaius dreams that Tiberius speaks these words to him: "One life and one death is appointed for us both, to spend the one and to meet the other in the service of the people" (Dryden's translation). Can you think of people in the Bible who were called to serve, and were told that it was them, not someone else, that God planned to use?

Lesson Four

Introduction

There was a rule among the Roman tribunes, that if even one of them disagreed with a proposal, the whole thing would be overthrown. Generally, this seemed to encourage teamwork and unanimity. But what could you do if a proposal was very, very important to you? And worse, what if the tribune disagreeing with you was also your friend?

Vocabulary

importunate: insistent

preferred: proposed

grateful: favourable

Saturn's temple: the public treasury

leave to exercise their office: refused to do their duties

changed their apparel: put on mourning clothes

the marketplace: the Roman Forum

voices: votes

a private man: someone with no position of authority

an enfranchised bondman: a servant whom he had made a free man

People

Marcus Octavius: he is said to be an ancestor of Gaius Octavius (Caesar Augustus, the first emperor of Rome)

Fulvius: not the same Fulvius mentioned later

Historic Occasions

133 B.C.: Marcus Octavius was deposed as tribune

Reading

Part One

Therefore, leaving to contrary and deny the law by argument, the rich men did put all their trust in **Marcus Octavius**, colleague and fellow tribune with Tiberius in office, who was a grave and wise young man, and Tiberius' very familiar friend. So that the first time they came to him, to oppose him against the confirmation of this law: he prayed them to hold him excused, because Tiberius was his very friend. But in the end, being compelled unto it through the great number of the rich men that were **importunate** with him: he did withstand Tiberius' law, which was enough to overthrow it. For if any one of the tribunes speak against it, though all the other[s] pass with it, he overthroweth it: because they all can do nothing, if one of them be against it.

Tiberius being very much offended with it, proceeded no further in this first [milder] law, and in a rage **preferred** another more **grateful** to the common people, as also more extreme against the rich. In that law he ordained that whosoever had any lands contrary to the ancient laws of Rome, that he should presently depart from them.

But thereupon there fell out continual brawls, in the pulpit for orations, against Octavius: in the which, though they were very earnest and vehement one against another, yet there passed no foul words from them, (how hot soever they were one with another) that should shame his companion.

[For not alone—

"In revellings and Bacchic play,"

147

but also in contentions and political animosities, a noble nature and a temperate education stay and compose the mind.]

Thereupon Tiberius finding that this law among others touched Octavius, because he enjoyed a great deal of land that was the commonwealth's: he prayed him secretly to contend no more against him, promising him to give him, of his own, the value of those lands which he should be driven to forsake, although he was not very able to perform it.

But when he saw Octavius would not be persuaded, he then **preferred** a law, that all magistrates and officers should cease their authority, till the law were either passed, or rejected, by voices of the people. [He further sealed up the gates of **Saturn's temple**, so that the treasurers could neither take any money out from thence, nor put any in], upon great penalties to be forfeited by the praetors or any other magistrate of authority that should break this order. Hereupon, all the magistrates fearing this penalty, did **leave to exercise their office** for the time. But then the rich men that were of great livings, **changed their apparel**, and walked very sadly up and down **the marketplace**, and laid [in] secret wait to take Tiberius, having hired men to kill him: which caused Tiberius himself, openly before them all, to wear a short dagger under his long gown, properly called in Latin, *Dolon*.

Part Two

When the day came that this law should be established, Tiberius called the people to give their **voices**: and the rich men on the other side, they took away the pots by force, wherein the papers of men's **voices** were thrown; [thus all things were in confusion]. For the faction of Tiberius was the stronger side, by the number of people that were gathered about him for that purpose: had it not been for Manlius and **Fulvius**, both the which had been consuls, who went unto him, and besought him with the tears in their eyes, and holding up their hands, that he would let the law alone. Tiberius thereupon, foreseeing the instant danger of some great mischief, as also for the reverence he bare unto two such noble persons, he stayed a little, and asked them what they would have him to do.

They made answer, that they were not able to counsel him in a matter of so great weight, but they prayed him notwithstanding, he would be contented to refer it to the judgement of the Senate. But afterwards perceiving that the Senate sat upon it, and had determined nothing, because the rich men were of too great authority: he entered into another [course] that was neither honest nor meet, which was, to deprive Octavius of his tribuneship, knowing that otherwise he could not possibly come to pass the law.

But before he took that course, he openly entreated [Octavius] in the face of the people with courteous words, and took him by the hand, and prayed him to stand no more against him, and to do the people this pleasure, which required a matter just and reasonable, and only requested this final recompense for the great pains they took in service abroad for their country. Octavius denied him plainly. Then said Tiberius openly, that both of them being [united in the same office, and of equal authority], this contention could not be possibly ended, without civil war: and that he could see no way to remedy it, unles one of them two were deposed from their office. Thereupon he bade Octavius [to summon the people and] begin first with him, and he would rise from the bench with a good will, and become **a private man**, if the people were so contented. Octavius would do nothing in it. [Tiberius then said he would himself put to the people the question of Octavius' deposition, if upon mature deliberation he did not alter his mind; and after this declaration, he adjourned the assembly till the next day.]

The next morning the people being again assembled, Tiberius going up to his seat, attempted again to persuade Octavius to leave off. [But all being to no purpose], he referred the matter to the **voice** of the people, whether they were contented Octavius should be deposed from his office. Now there were five and thirty tribes of the people, of the which, seventeen of them had already passed their voices against Octavius, so that there remained but one tribe more to put him out of his office. Then Tiberius made them stay for proceeding any further, and prayed Octavius again, embracing him before all the people, with all the entreaty possible: that for self-will's sake he would not suffer such an open shame to be done unto him, as to be put out of his office: neither also to make him the occasion and instrument of so pitiful a deed.

They say that Octavius at this last entreaty was somewhat moved and won by his persuasions, and that weeping, he stayed a long time, and made no answer. But when he looked upon the rich men that stood in a great company together, he was ashamed (I think) to have their ill wills, and rather betook himself to the loss of his office, and so bade Tiberius do what he would. Thereupon [Octavius] being deprived by [the] voices of the people, Tiberius commanded one of his **enfranchised bondmen** to pull him out of the pulpit for orations: for he used [them] instead of sergeants. This made the sight so much more lamentable, to see Octavius thus shamefully plucked away by force. Yea, furthermore, the common people would have run upon him, but the rich men came to rescue him, and would not suffer [them] to do him further hurt. So Octavius saved himself, running away alone, after he had been rescued thus from the fury of the people.

Narration and Discussion

Discuss this passage from **Part One**: "yet there passed no foul words from them, (how hot soever they were one with another) that should shame his companion." How can a noble nature and a temperate education help us during times of disagreement as well as during the pleasant times (the revellings)?

This would be a good time to review the introductory note about the sanctity of tribunes. If they were considered untouchable, not to be interfered with, why did Tiberius break that tradition? Should he have handled the conflict differently?

Lesson Five

Introduction

With Octavius out of the way, Tiberius felt free to proceed with his plans; and when a large royal inheritance came into the Roman treasury, he knew just what should be done with it. However, his zeal for the poor, and his dislike for bureaucratic red tape and procedure, made some of his colleagues more uncomfortable than ever.

Vocabulary

commissioners: If you think it's odd that Tiberius was serving on his own land commission, you're not alone.

obulus, pl. **obuli:** a silver coin

preferred a law immediately: Such a financial proposal should have been made by the senators, not by a tribune

tillage: farm land

a magistrate: referring to Marcus Octavius

ran to his fine subtle questions: tried to trap people with questions

gravelled: Dryden, "disconcerted"

lewd: bad, wicked

when he list: when he chooses

Vestal Nuns: Vestal Virgins (a religious order for women)

apology: justification for his actions

People

Publius Nasica: Publius Cornelius Scipio Nasica Serapio, a cousin of the Gracchi; *Pontifex Maximus* in 141 B.C., consul in 138 B.C.

Attalus, surnamed Philopater: Attalus III Philometor Euergetes (c. 170 B.C.—133 B.C.), king of Pergamon

Eudemus [the] Pergamenian: an official from Pergamon

Reading

After that, the Law Agraria passed for division of lands, and three **commissioners** were appointed to make inquiry and distribution thereof. The commissioners appointed were these: Tiberius himself; Appius Claudius, his father-in-law; and Gaius Gracchus his brother; who was not at that time in Rome, but [was] in the camp with Scipio

Africanus [*the Younger*], at the siege of the city of Numantia. Thus Tiberius very quietly passed over these matters, and no man durst withstand him: and furthermore, he substituted in Octavius' place no man of quality, but only one of his followers, called Mucius.

Wherewith the noble men were so sore offended with him, that fearing the increase of his greatness, [they took all opportunities of affronting him publicly in the Senate house]. For when Tiberius demanded a tent at the charge of the commonwealth, when he should go abroad to make division of these lands, as they usually granted unto others, that many times went in far meaner commissions: they flatly denied him, and only granted him nine of their **obuli** a day for his ordinary allowance. [The chief promoter of these affronts was **Publius Nasica**, who openly abandoned himself to his feelings of hatred against Tiberius, being a large holder of the public lands, and not a little resenting now to be turned out of them by force.]

But the people, on the other [hand], were all in an uproar against the rich. Insomuch as one of Tiberius' friends being dead upon the sudden, upon whose body being dead there appeared [malignant-looking spots]: the common people ran suddenly to his burial, and cried out that he was poisoned. And so taking up the bier (whereon his body lay) upon their shoulders, they were present at the fire of his funerals, where immediately appeared certain signs to make them suspect that, indeed, there was vehement cause of presumption he was poisoned.

[*Other strange phenomena also took place.*]

Tiberius put on mourning apparel, and brought his sons before [the people], and besought the people to be good unto them and their mother, as one that despaired of his health and safety.

About that time died **Attalus, surnamed Philopater,** and **Eudemus [the] Pergamenian** brought his will to Rome, in the which he made the people of Rome his heirs. Wherefore Tiberius, still to increase the goodwill of the common people towards him, **preferred a law immediately**, that the ready money that came by the inheritance of this king should be distributed among the poor citizens, on whose lot it should fall to have any part of the division of the lands of the commonwealth; to furnish them towards house, and to set up their **tillage.** Furthermore, he said, that concerning the towns and cities of the kingdom of Attalus, the Senate had nothing to do to take any order with them, but that the people were to dispose of them, and that he himself would put it out. That made him again more hated of the Senate than before, insomuch as there was one Pompeius, a senator, that standing up, said that he was next neighbour unto Tiberius, and that by reason of his neighbourhood he knew that Eudemus had given him one of King Attalus' royal bands, with a purple gown besides, for a token that he should one day be king of Rome.

And Quintus Metellus also reproved him, for that [in the days that Tiberius Senior was] censor, the Romans having supped in the town, and repairing every man home to his house, they did put out their torches and lights, because men seeing them return, they should not think they tarried too long in company banqueting: and that [now], in contrary manner, the seditious and needy rabble of the common people did light his son [*Tiberius Junior*] home, and accompany him all night long up and down the town.

At that time there was one Titus Annius, a man that had no goodness nor honesty in him, howbeit [he was] taken for a great reasoner, and for a subtle questioner and answerer. He provoked Tiberius to answer him, [declaring him to have deposed **a magistrate** who by law was sacred and inviolable]. The people took this provocation very angrily, and Tiberius also coming out, and having assembled the people, commanded them to bring this Annius before him, that he might be indicted in the marketplace. But he finding himself far inferior unto Tiberius, both in dignity and eloquence, **ran to his fine subtle questions**: and prayed Tiberius before he did proceed to his accusation, that he would first answer him to a question he would ask him. Tiberius bade him say what he would. So silence being made, Annius asked him: "If thou wouldst defame me, and offer me injury, and that I called one of thy [colleagues] to help me, and he should rise to take my part, and anger thee: wouldst thou therefore put him out of his office?"

It is reported that Tiberius was so **gravelled** with this question, that though he was one of the readiest speakers, and the boldest in his orations of any man: yet at that time he held his peace, and had no power to speak, and therefore he presently dismissed the assembly.

[But beginning to understand] that of all the things he did, the deposing of Octavius from his office was thought (not only of the nobility, but of the common people also) as foul and willful a part as ever he played, for that thereby he had imbased, and utterly overthrown the dignity of the tribunes, the which was always had in great veneration until that present time. To excuse himself therefore, he made an excellent oration to the people, whereby shall appear unto you some special points thereof, to discern the better the force and effect of his eloquence.

"The tribuneship," said he, "indeed was a holy and sacred thing, as particularly consecrated to the people, and established for their benefit and safety: where contrariwise, if the tribune do offer the people any wrong, he thereby [di]minisheth their power, and taketh away the means from them to declare their wills by voices. Besides that, he doth also imbase his own authority, leaving to do the thing for the which his authority first was given him. Or otherwise we could not choose but suffer a tribune, if it pleased him, to overthrow the Capitol, or to set fire [to] the arsenal: and yet notwithstanding this wicked part, if it were committed, he should be tribune of the people still, though a **lewd** tribune. But when he goeth about to take away the authority and power of the people, then he is no more a tribune. Were not this against all reason, think you, that a tribune **when he list**, may take a consul, and commit him to prison: and that the people should not withstand the authority of the tribune, who gave him the same, when he would use his authority to the prejudice of the people? For the people are they that do choose both consul and tribune. Furthermore, the kingly dignity (because in the same is contained the absolute authority and power of all other kinds of magistrates and offices together) is consecrated with very great and holy ceremonies, drawing very near unto the godhead: and yet the people expulsed King Tarquin, because he used his authority with cruelty, and for the injury he offered one man only,

154

the most ancient rule and government, (by the which the foundation of Rome was first laid) was utterly abolished.

"And who is there in all the city of Rome to be reckoned so holy as the **Vestal Nuns**, which have the custody and keeping of the everlasting fire? And yet if [one of these transgress], she is buried alive for her offence: for when they are not holy to the gods, they lose the liberty they have, in respect of serving the gods. Even so also it is unmeet, that the tribune, if he offend the people, should for the people's sake be reverenced any more: seeing that through his own folly he hath deprived himself of that authority they gave him. And if it be so that he was chosen tribune by the most part of the tribes of the people: then by greater reason is he justly deprived, that by [the general consent of them all] he is forsaken and deposed.

"There is nothing more holy nor inviolate, than things offered up unto the gods: and yet it was never seen that any man did forbid the people to take them, to remove and transport them from place to place, as they thought good. Even so, they may as lawfully transfer the office of the tribune unto any other, as any other offering consecrated to the gods.

"Furthermore, it is manifest that any officer or magistrate may lawfully depose himself: for, it hath been often seen, that men in office have [of their own act surrendered and desired to be discharged from."

[These were the principal heads of Tiberius' **apology**.]

Narration and Discussion

Why were the senators so eager to re-open the issue of Octavius at this time?

Can you put Tiberius' speech in your own words? Had Octavius actually violated his oath?

For older students: It is not difficult to understand the Romans' fear of "kings," and their nervousness about those who seemed overly ambitious for power and position. They even had a word for those who leaned towards sole government control: *regnum*, or monarchism. What is harder for us to wrap our non-Roman minds around is their suspicion of anyone who seemed to be too interested in the problems of the poor. Can you follow their thinking on this? How did that put Tiberius in a difficult position? As an extension, consider how this view contrasts with the teachings of Christ, and with Old Testament passages such as Isaiah 58:6-9.

Lesson Six

Introduction

Tiberius was informed that there were finally enough supporters assembled to pass the laws he had proposed, and he headed for the Capitol. Because of extreme mis-communication during the assembly, a group of senators, protesting the refusal of the consul to have Tiberius arrested, incited a riot.

Vocabulary

Roman knights: those of the "Equestrian Class" or Equites, aristocrats ranking below the Patricians

imbase: lower, decrease

the voices of the people: he needed to have a large number of the common people present (those who agreed with his proposals) in order to pass the new laws

cast them down meat: gave them chicken feed

stayed: in this context, it means worried, gave pause to

press: crowd

girt their long gowns unto them: tucked up their togas

truncheons: clubs

required: requested

they fell one on anothers' neck[s] for haste: that is, in trying to get out of their way

hied them apace: hurried

coat: tunic

staves and stones: Dryden, "clubs and staves"

Reading

Part One

Now his friends perceiving the threats the rich and noble men gave out against him, they wished him, for the safety of his person, to make suit to be tribune again the next year. Whereupon he began to flatter the common people again afresh, by new laws which he preferred: by the which he took away the time and number of years prescribed when every citizen of Rome was bound to go to the wars, being called, and his name billed.

He made it lawful also for men to appeal from sentence of the judges unto the people, and thrust in also amongst the senators (which then had absolute authority to judge among themselves) a like number of the **Roman knights**; and by this means sought to weaken and **imbase** the authority of the Senate, increasing also the power of the people, more of malice than any reason, or for any justice or benefit to the commonwealth. Furthermore, when it came to the gathering of **the voices of the people** for the confirmation of his new laws, finding that his enemies were the stronger in the assembly, because all the people were not yet come together: he fell a-quarrelling with his brethren the tribunes, always to win time, and yet in the end brake up the assembly, commanding them to return the next morning.

There he would be the first man in the marketplace, apparelled all in black, his face beblubbered with tears, and looking heavily upon the matter, praying the people assembled to have compassion upon him, saying, that he was afraid lest his enemies would come in the night, and overthrow his house to kill him. Thereupon the people were so moved withal, that many of them came and brought their tents, and lay about his house to watch it. At the break of the day, the keeper of the chickens, by signs of the which they do divine of things to come, brought them unto him, and **cast them down meat** before them. None of them would come out of the cage but one only, and yet with much ado, shaking the cage: and when it came out, it would eat no **meat**, but only lift up her left wing, and put forth her leg, and so ran into the cage again. This sign made Tiberius remember another he had had before. He had a marvellous fair helmet and very rich, which he wore in the wars: under it were crept two snakes unawares to any, and [they] laid eggs, and hatched them. This made Tiberius wonder the more, because of the ill signs of the chickens.

Notwithstanding, he went out of his house, when he heard that the people were assembled in the Capitol, but as he went out, he hit his foot such a blow against a stone at the threshold of the door, that he broke the nail of his great toe, which fell in such a-bleeding, that it bled through his shoe. Again, he had not gone far, but he saw upon the top of a house on his left hand, a couple of ravens fighting together: and notwithstanding that there passed a great number of people by, yet a stone which one of these ravens cast from them, came and fell hard at Tiberius' foot. The fall thereof **stayed** the stoutest man he had about him. But Blossius, the philosopher of Cumes that did accompany him, told him it were a great shame for him, and enough to kill the hearts of all his followers: that Tiberius being the son of Gracchus, and [grandson] of Scipio Africanus, and the chief man besides of all the people's side, for fear of a raven, should not obey his citizens that called him: and how that his enemies and ill-willers would not make a laughing sport of it, but would plainly tell the people that this was a trick of a tyrant that reigned indeed, and that for pride and disdain did abuse the people's goodwills. Furthermore, divers messengers came unto him, and said that his friends that were in the Capitol sent to pray him to make haste, for all went well with him.

Part Two

When he came thither, he was honourably received: for the people seeing him coming, cried out for joy to welcome him, and when he was gotten up to his feet, they shewed themselves both careful and loving towards him, looking warily that none came near him, but such as they knew well. While Mutius began again to call the tribes of the people to give their voices, he could not proceed according to the accustomed order, for the great noise the hindmost people made, thrusting forward, and being driven back, and one mingling with another.

In the meantime, Flavius Flaccus, one of the senators, got up into a place where all the people might see him, and when he saw that his voice could not be heard [by] Tiberius, he made a sign with his hand that he had some matter of great importance to tell him. Tiberius straight bade them make a lane through the **press**. So with much ado, Flavius came at length unto him, and told him that the rich men [seeing they could not prevail upon the consul to espouse their quarrel], determined themselves to come and kill him, having a great number of their friends and bondmen armed for the purpose.

Tiberius immediately declared this conspiracy unto his friends and followers: who straight **girt their long gowns unto them**, and broke the sergeants' javelins which they carried in their hands to make room among the people, and took the **truncheons** of the same to resist those that would set upon them. The people also that stood furthest off, marvelled at it, and asked what the matter was. Tiberius by a sign to tell them the danger he was in, laid both his hands on his head, because they could not hear his voice for the great noise they made. His enemies seeing the sign he gave, ran presently to the Senate, crying out that Tiberius **required** a royal band or diadem of the people, and that it was an evident sign, because they saw him clap his hands upon his head. This tale troubled all the company.

Whereupon Nasica besought the consul, chief of the Senate, to help the commonwealth, and to take away this tyrant. The consul gently answered again, that he would use no force, neither put any citizen to death, but lawfully condemned: as also he would not receive Tiberius, nor protect him, if the people by his persuasion or commandment, should commit any act contrary to the law.

Nasica then rising in anger, "Since the matter is so," said he, "that the consul regardeth not the commonwealth: all you then, that will defend the authority of the law, follow me." Thereupon he cast the skirt of his gown over his head, and went straight to the Capitol. They that followed him also took their gowns, and wrapped them about their arms, and [forced their way after him]; and yet very few of the people durst meet with such states as they were to stay them, because they were the chiefest men of the city, but every man fleeing from them, **they fell one on anothers' neck[s] for haste.** They that followed them, had brought from home great levers and clubs, and as they went, they took up feet of trestles and chairs which the people had overthrown and broken, running away; and **hied them apace** to meet with Tiberius, striking at them that stood in their way: so that in short space they had dispersed all the common people, and many were slain, fleeing.

Tiberius seeing that, betook him to his legs to save himself, but as he was fleeing, one took him by the gown, and stayed him: but he, leaving his gown behind him, ran in his **coat**, and running, fell upon them that were down before. So as he was rising up again, the first man that struck him, and that was plainly seen [to] strike him, was one of the tribunes his brethren, called Publius Satureius, who gave him a great rap on the head with the foot of a chair; and the second [*fatal*] blow he had was given him by Lucius Rufus, that boasted of it as if he had done a notable act.

In this tumult, there were slain above three hundred men, and [they] were all killed with **staves and stones**, and not one man [was] hurt with any iron.

Narration and Discussion

In **Part One**, what were some of the new laws that Tiberius proposed? What was the purpose of his dramatics in the forum? Did Tiberius really believe that he was in danger?

How does **Part Two** parallel the *Life of Julius Caesar*? Can you predict how the people of Rome would react to the death of Tiberius and so many others?

Lesson Seven

Introduction

After the riot and the death of Tiberius Gracchus, Rome was in shock. According to Plutarch, it was "the first sedition among the citizens of Rome that fell out with murder and bloodshed, since the expulsion of the kings." Who was at fault? Was it safer to support Tiberius, or to say that he had brought his fate on himself?

Vocabulary

sedition: uprising, rebellion

since the expulsion of the kings: in the entire history of the Roman Republic

commodity: benefit

law Agraria: law regarding the distribution of land (see introductory notes)

lands of the commonwealth: Roman territory

did presently threaten Nasica to accuse him: Dryden, "he was threatened with impeachment"

round: blunt, plainspoken

imbrued (or **embrued**): stained (i.e. with blood)

chief Bishop of Rome: *Pontifex Maximus*

churlishly: rudely

Life of Scipio: this no longer exists

meanly: plainly, simply

preferred: proposed

sloth and curiosity: Dryden: "a lazy retirement and effeminacy"; this archaic meaning of **curiosity** means being overly fastidious, too concerned with the small details of personal comfort or pleasure

covetous mind of getting: interest in personal gain

to practise in the commonwealth: to act as legal counsel in Rome or its provinces and colonies

he had such an eloquent tongue: he was so well-spoken

all the orators besides: the other speakers

it behoved them: it was necessary

treasurer: quaestor (see introductory notes for *Julius Caesar*)

martial: military

prayed his furtherance: wanted his help

predestined: fated or designed before birth

People

Publius Crassus: see **Lesson Three**

Fulvius: it's not clear which Fulvius this is

Historic Occasions

126 B.C.: Gaius Gracchus was chosen quaestor

Reading

Part One

This was the first **sedition** among the citizens of Rome that fell out with murder and bloodshed, **since the expulsion of the kings**. But for all other former dissensions (which were no trifles) they were easily pacified, either party giving place to other: the Senate for fear of the commoners, and the people for reverence they bare to the Senate. And it seemeth, that Tiberius himself would easily have yielded also, if they had proceeded by fair means and persuasion, so they had meant good faith, and would have killed no man: for at that time he had not, in all, above 3,000 men of the people about him. But surely it seems this conspiracy was executed against him more for [the] very spite and malice the rich men did bear him, than for any other apparent cause they presupposed against him.

For proof hereof may be alleged, the barbarous cruelty they used to his body, being dead. For they would not suffer his own brother to have his body to bury it by night, who made earnest suit unto them for it: but they threw him amongst the other bodies into the river.

Blossius also, the philosopher of Cuma, was brought before the consuls, and examined about this matter: who boldly confessed unto them, that he did as much as Tiberius commanded him. When Nasica did ask him, "And what if he had commanded thee to set fire on the Capitol?" he [gave] answer, that Tiberius would never have given him any such commandment. And when divers others also were still in hand with him about that question: "But if he had commanded thee?" "I would sure have done it," said he. "For he would never have commanded me to have done it, if it had not been for the **commodity** of the people." Thus he [e]scaped at that time, and afterwards fled into Asia unto Aristonicus, [and when Aristonicus was overthrown and ruined, killed himself].

Now the Senate, to pacify the people at that present time, did no more withstand the **law Agraria**, for division of the **lands of the commonwealth**, but suffered the people to appoint another commissioner for that purpose, in Tiberius' place. Thereupon **Publius Crassus** was chosen, being allied unto Tiberius, for Gaius Gracchus (Tiberius' brother) had married his daughter Licinia. Yet Cornelius Nepos sayeth, that it was not Crassus' daughter Gaius married, but the daughter of Brutus, that triumphed for the Lusitanians. Howbeit the best writers and authority agree with that [which] we write. But whatsoever was done, the people were marvellously offended with his death, and men might easily perceive, that they looked but for time and opportunity to be revenged, and **did presently threaten Nasica to accuse him**. [The Senate, therefore, fearing lest some mischief should befall him, sent him ambassador into Asia, though there was no occasion for his going thither.] For the common people did not dissemble the malice they bare him when they met him, but were very **round** with him, and called him tyrant, and murderer, excommunicate, and wicked man, that had **imbrued** his hands in the blood of the holy tribune, and within the most sacred temple of all the city. So in the end he was enforced to forsake Rome, though by his office he was bound to solemnize all the greatest sacrifices, because he was then **chief Bishop of Rome**. Thus, travelling out of his country like a mean man, and troubled in his mind: he died shortly after [*in 132 B.C.*], not far from the city of Pergamum.

[Sidebar: the reaction of Scipio Africanus [the Younger] to the death of Tiberius.]

Truly it is not greatly to be wondered at, though the people so much hated Nasica, considering that Scipio Africanus (whom the people of Rome for juster causes had loved better than any man else whatsoever) was like to have lost all the people's goodwills they bare him, because that being at the siege of Numantia, when news was brought him of Tiberius' death, he [repeated] this verse of Homer:

> Such end upon him ever light / Which in such
> doings doth delight.

Furthermore, being asked in the assembly of the people, by Gaius and **Fulvius**, what he thought of Tiberius' death: he answered them, that he did not like his doings. After that the people handled him very **churlishly**, and did ever break off his oration, which they never did before: and he himself also would revile the people even in the assembly. [But of this the particulars are given in the *Life of Scipio*.]

Part Two

Now Gaius Gracchus at the first, because he feared the enemies of his dead brother, or otherwise for that he sought means to make them more hated of the people: he absented himself for a time out of the common assembly, and kept at home and meddled not, as a man contented to live **meanly**, without busying himself in the commonwealth: insomuch as he made men think and report both, that he did utterly mislike those matters which his brother had **preferred**. Howbeit he was then but a young man, and nine years younger than his brother Tiberius, who was not thirty years old when he was slain.

But in process of time, he made his manners and conditions (by little and little) appear, [*that he was one*] who hated **sloth and curiosity**, and was least of all given unto any **covetous mind of getting**: for he gave himself to be eloquent, as preparing him wings afterwards **to practise in the commonwealth**. So that it appeared plainly, that when time came, he would not stand still, and look on.

When one Vectius, a friend of his, was sued, he took upon him to defend his cause in court. The people that were present, and heard him speak, they leaped for joy to see him: for **he had such an eloquent tongue**, that **all the orators besides** were but children to him. Hereupon the rich men began to be afraid again, and whispered among themselves, that **it behoved them** to beware he came not to be tribune.

It chanced so that he was chosen **treasurer**, and it was his fortune to go into the Isle of Sardinia, with the consul Orestes. His enemies were glad of that, and he himself was not sorry for it. For he was a **martial** man, and as skillful in arms, as he was else an excellent orator: but yet he was afraid to come into the pulpit for orations, and misliked to deal in matters of state, albeit he could not altogether deny the people, and his friends that **prayed his furtherance**. For this cause therefore he was very glad of this voyage, that he might absent himself for a time out of Rome: though [*some*] were of opinion that he was more popular, and desirous of the common people's good will and favour, than his brother had been before him. But indeed he was clean contrary: for it appeared that at the first he was drawn rather against his will, than of any special desire he had to deal in the commonwealth.

Cicero the orator also sayeth, that Gaius was bent altogether to flee from office in the commonwealth, and to live quietly as a private man. But Tiberius (Gaius' brother) appeared to him in his sleep, and calling him by his name, said unto him: "Brother, why dost thou prolong time, for thou canst not possibly escape? For we were both **predestined** to one manner of life and death, for procuring the benefit of the people."

Narration and Discussion

Did Nasica deserve the treatment he received?

Why did Gaius live so quietly for awhile, even against his own natural gifts and interests? How did he need to prepare before taking up his brother's causes? You may wish to go back to the profile of Gaius that you wrote in **Lesson One**.

Do you see any parallels here to the early life of Moses? Can you think of any other reluctant leaders in history or literature?

What qualities did Gaius display that made rich men afraid of him, but made other people desire his leadership?

How might the study of eloquence give one wings?

Lesson Eight

Introduction

Like his brother before him, Gaius Gracchus sometimes did the right things in wrong ways, or at least in ways that created jealousy or suspicion. In this lesson, the problem was one of supplies for the army. Who sent them, in Gaius' opinion, was not as important as keeping the soldiers fed; what did it matter if they came from a foreign king who "owed him one?" But Gaius showed himself surprisingly able to put this kind of trouble in its place. Maybe things would go better this time around.

Vocabulary

painfulness: Gaius was painstaking, hardworking

corn: grain, food supplies

to continue Gaius their treasurer: Gaius (as quaestor to Orestes) would be required to remain in Sardinia

in choler: in a rage

Field of Mars: the *Campus Martius*, a large area which at this time was open space used for political or military events. Later, parts of the land were sold to private owners, and buildings were erected on it such as the Pantheon.

let: prevent

the examples of their ancestors: that is, in their respect for and protection of tribunes, and Roman citizens in general

should pertain to the people: the citizens should have a say in it

the lands of the commonwealth: Roman territory

judgement: the courts of justice

honoured and feared: Dryden says "dreaded"

Roman knights: see previous lessons

Comitium: an open-air meeting space in the Roman Forum

People

King Micipsa: the king of Numidia, who had a friendly relationship with Gaius Gracchus

Popilius: Publius Popillius Laenas, consul in 132 B.C., but praetor during the events of 133

Historic Occasions

123 and 122 B.C.: Gaius Gracchus was tribune

Reading

Part One

Now when Gaius arrived in Sardinia [*as quaestor*], he shewed all the proofs that might be in a valiant man, and excelled all the young men of his age, in hardiness against his enemies, in justice to his inferiors, and in love and obedience towards the consul his captain: but in temperance, sobriety, and in **painfulness**, he excelled all them that were elder than he.

The winter by chance fell out very sharp, and full of sickness in Sardinia: whereupon the consul sent into the cities to help his soldiers with some clothes: but the towns sent in post to Rome, to pray the

Senate they might be discharged of that burden. The Senate found their allegation reasonable, whereupon they wrote to the consul to find some other means to clothe his people. The consul could make no other shift for them, and so the poor soldiers in the meantime smarted for it. But Gaius Gracchus went himself unto the cities and so persuaded them, that they of themselves sent to the Romans' camp such things as they lacked. This being carried to Rome, it was thought straight it was a pretty beginning to creep into the peoples' favour, and indeed it [raised new jealousies among the senators]. In the neck of that, there arrived ambassadors of Africa at Rome, sent from **King Micipsa**, who told the Senate that the king their master, for Gaius Gracchus' sake, had sent their army **corn** into Sardinia.

The senators were so offended withal, that they thrust the ambassadors out of the Senate, and so gave order that other soldiers should be sent in their places that were in Sardinia: and that Orestes should still remain consul there, meaning also **to continue Gaius their treasurer**. But when he [Gaius] heard of it, he straight took sea, and returned to Rome **in choler**.

When men saw Gaius returned to Rome unlooked for, he was reproved for it not only by his enemies, but by the common people also: who thought his return very strange before his captain, under whom he was treasurer. He being accused hereof before the censors, prayed he might be heard.

So, answering his accusation, he so turned the people's minds that heard him, that they all said he had [*been wronged*]. For he told them, that he had served twelve years in the wars, where others were enforced to remain but ten years: and that he had continued treasurer under his captain, the space of three years, where the law gave him liberty to return at the end of the year. And that he alone of all men else that had been in the wars, had carried his purse full, and brought it home empty: where others having drunk the wine which they carried thither in vessels, had afterwards brought them home full of gold and silver.

Afterwards they [*also accused*] him as accessory to a conspiracy, that was revealed in the city of Fregellae. But having cleared all that suspicion, and being discharged, he presently made suit to be tribune: wherein he had all the men of quality his sworn enemies. On the other side also he had so great favour of the common people, that there came men out of all parts of Italy to be at his election, and that such a number of them, as there was no lodging to be had for them all. Furthermore, the **Field of Mars** not being large enough to hold such a multitude of people, there were that gave their voices upon the top of houses.

Now the noblemen could no otherwise **let** the people of their will, nor prevent Gaius of his hope, but where he thought to be the first tribune, he was only pronounced the fourth. But when he was once [in office], he became immediately the chief man, because he was as eloquent as any man of his time. And furthermore, he had a large occasion of calamity offered him: which made him bold to speak, bewailing the death of his brother. For what matters soever he spake of, he always fell in talk of that, remembering them what matters had passed: and laying before them **the examples of their ancestors:** who in old time had made war with the Phalisces [*Falerii*], by the means of one Genutius, tribune of the people, unto whom they [the Phalisces] had offered injury: who also did condemn Gaius Veturius to death, [for refusing to give way in the Forum to a tribune].

> "Where[as] these," said he, "that standing before you in sight, have slain my brother Tiberius with staves, and have dragged his body from the Mount of the Capitol, all the city over, to throw it into the river: and with him also have most cruelly slain all his friends they could come by, without any law or justice at all. And yet by an ancient custom of long time observed in this city of Rome, when any man is accused of treason, and that of duty he must appear at the time appointed him: they do notwithstanding in the morning send a trumpet to his house, to summon him to appear: and moreover the Judges were not wont to condemn him, before this ceremony was performed: so careful and respective were our predecessors, where it touched the life of any Roman."

Part Two

Now Gaius having first stirred up the people with these persuasions (for he had a marvellous loud voice) he preferred two laws. The first, that [*anyone*] that had once been put out of office by the people, should never after be capable of any other office. The second, that if any consul had banished any citizen without [a legal trial], the sentence and hearing of the matter **should pertain to the people**.

The first of these two laws did plainly defame Octavius, whom Tiberius his brother had by the people deposed from the tribuneship. The second also touched **Popilius**, who being praetor [*at the time*], had banished his brother Tiberius' friends. [Whereupon Popilius, being unwilling to stand the hazard of a trial, fled out of Italy].

And touching the first law, Gaius himself did afterwards revoke it, declaring unto the people, that he [yielded in the case of] Octavius at the request of his mother Cornelia. The people were very glad of it, and confirmed it, honouring her no less for respect of her sons, than also for Scipio's sake her father. For afterwards they cast her image in brass, and set it up with this inscription: "Cornelia, the mother of the Gracchi." Many common matters are found written, touching Cornelia his mother and eloquently pleaded in her behalf, by Gaius against her adversaries. As when he said unto one of them: "How darest thou presume to speak evil of Cornelia, that had Tiberius to her son?" Thus were Gaius' words sharp and stinging, and many such like are to be gathered out of his writings.

Furthermore, he [proposed] many other laws afterwards to increase the people's authority, and to imbase the Senate's greatness. The first was, for the restoring of the colonies to Rome, in dividing **the lands of the commonwealth** unto the poor citizens that should inhabit there. The other, that they should apparel the soldiers at the charge of the commonwealth, and that it should not be deducted out of their pay: and also, that no citizen should be [obliged] to serve in the wars, under seventeen years of age at the least.

Another law was, for their confederates of Italy: that through all Italy they should have as free voices in the election of any magistrate, as the natural citizens of Rome itself.

Another setting a reasonable price of the corn that should be distributed unto the poor people.

Another touching **judgement**, whereby he did greatly [di]minish the authority of the Senate. For before, the senators were [*the*] only judges of all matters, which made them to be the more **honoured and feared** of the people and the **Roman knights**: and now he joined three hundred Roman knights unto the other three hundred senators, and brought it so to pass, that all matters judicial should be equally judged among those six hundred men.

After he had passed this law, it is reported he [showed unusual earnestness] in observing all other things, but this one thing specially: that where all other orators speaking to the people turned them[selves] towards the palace where the senators sat, and to that side of the marketplace which is called **Comitium**: he in contrary manner when he made his oration, turned him outwards towards the other side of the marketplace, and after that kept it constantly, and never failed. Thus, by a little turning and altering of his look only, he removed a great matter. For he so transferred all the government of the commonwealth from the Senate, unto the judgement of the people: to teach the orators by his example, that in their orations they should behold the people, not the Senate.

Narration and Discussion

Compare the description of Gaius in the first paragraph with what we have been previously told of him. Does it sound like he has changed?

Why did the announcement by the African ambassadors cause so much upset? Which was more important: that the army get supplies, or that the right people get credit for it?

How did Gaius successfully defend himself on his return from Sardinia?

Gaius changed the direction in which he gave his speeches. Why did this signal a literal change of direction for the government?

Lesson Nine

Introduction

"Now, the people having not only confirmed the law he made touching the judges, but given him also full power and authority to choose among the Roman knights such judges as he liked of: he found thereby he had absolute power in his own hands, insomuch as the senators themselves did ask counsel of him." Gaius used his power to build mend roads, re-people colonies, and refuse tribute from Spain that would impoverish the people there. But by **Part Two** of this lesson, admiration was turning to jealousy, and a conspiracy arose against him.

Vocabulary

matters meet for their honour: suitable to their importance

a good and honourable act: not the sending of the wheat, but Gaius' refusal of it

garners: storage barns

estate: dignity

a stately man, and very cruel: proud and violent

cawcie: the word is more familiar in the form "causeway," which is a road made across a marsh; but it can also mean a paved highway

line or plummet: measuring devices

he cared not much: Dryden, "he would never blame them for the refusal"

to further his suit: to promote Gaius Fannius

the freedom of Rome: the privileges of citizenship

playing the demagogue: trying to get votes or support by appealing to people's emotions and prejudices

People

Fabius [the] vicepraetor: Quintus Fabius Maximus Allobrogicus, the governor of Spain in 123 B.C., and consul two years later

Gaius Fannius: Gaius Fannius Strabo, elected consul for 122 B.C.

Livius Drusus: Marcus Livius Drusus, appointed tribune for the sole purpose of counter-offering anything that Gaius Gracchus proposed (although his own proposals were never meant to be carried out).

Reading

Part One

Now, the people having not only confirmed the law he made touching the judges, but given him also full power and authority to choose among the Roman knights such judges as he liked of: he found thereby he had absolute power in his own hands, insomuch as the senators themselves did ask counsel of him. So did he ever give good counsel, and did prefer **matters meet for their honour**.

As amongst others, the law he made touching certain wheat that **Fabius [the] vicepraetor** had sent out of Spain: which was **a good and honourable act**. He persuaded the Senate that the corn might be sold, and so to send back again the money thereof unto the towns and cities from whence the corn came: and [that they should] punish Fabius [because] he made the empire of Rome hateful and intolerable unto the provinces and subjects of the same. This matter won him great love and commendation of all the provinces subject to Rome. Furthermore, he made laws for the restoring of the decayed towns, for mending of highways, for building of **garners** for provision of corn.

And to bring all these things to pass, he himself took upon him the only care and enterprise, being never wearied with any pains taken in ordering of so great affairs. For, he followed all those things so earnestly and effectually, as if he had had but one master in hand: insomuch that they who most hated and feared him, wondered most to see his diligence and quick dispatch in matters.

The people also wondered much to behold him only, seeing always such a number of labourers, artificers, ambassadors, officers, soldiers, and learned men, whom he easily satisfied and dispatched, keeping still his **estate**, and yet using great courtesy and civility, entertaining every one of them privately: so that he made his accusers to be found liars, that said he was **a stately man, and very cruel**. Thus he won the good will of the common people, being more popular and familiar in his conversation and deeds, than he was otherwise in his orations.

But the greatest pains and care he took upon him was in seeing the highways mended, the which he would have as well done, as profitably done. For he would cast the **cawcies** by the line in the softest ground in the fields, and then would pave them with hard stone, and cast a great deal of gravel upon it, which he caused to be brought thither. When he found any low or watery places which the rivers had eaten into, he raised them up, or else made bridges over them, with an even height equal to either side of the **cawcie**: so that all his work carried a goodly level withal even by the **line or plummet**, which was a pleasure to behold it. Furthermore, he divided these highways by miles, every mile containing eight furlongs, and at every mile's end, he set up a stone for a mark. At either end also of these highways thus paved, he set certain stones of convenient height [at small distances from one another], to help the travellers-by to take their horses' backs again, without any help.

The people for these things highly praising and extolling him, and being ready to make shew of their love and goodwill to him any manner of way: he told them openly one day in his oration, that he had a request to make unto them, the which if it would please them to grant him, he would think they did him a marvellous pleasure: and if they denied him also, **he cared not much**. Then every man thought it was the consulship he meant to ask, and that he would sue to be tribune and consul together. But when the day came to choose the consuls, every man looking attentively what he would do: they marvelled when they saw him come down the Field of Mars, and brought **Gaius Fannius** with his friends, **to further his suit** for the consulship. Therein he served Fannius' turn, for he was presently chosen consul: and Gaius Gracchus was the second time chosen tribune again, not of his own suit, but by the goodwill of the people.

Part Two

Gaius, perceiving that the senators were his open enemies, and that Fannius the consul was but a slack friend unto him, he began again to curry favour with the common people, and to prefer new laws, setting forth the law of the colonies, that they should send [some] of the poor citizens to replenish the cities of Tarentum and Capua; and that they should grant all the Latins **the freedom of Rome**. The Senate perceiving his power grew great, and that in the end he would be so strong that they could not withstand him: they devised a new and strange way to pluck the people's goodwill from him, [by **playing the demagogue** in opposition to him, and offering favours contrary to all good policy].

There was one of the tribunes, a brother in office with Gaius, called **Livius Drusus**, a man nobly born, and as well brought up as any other Roman: who for wealth and eloquence was not inferior to the greatest men of estimation in Rome. The chiefest senators went unto him, and persuaded him to take part with them against Gaius, not to use any force or violence against the people to withstand them in anything, but contrarily [by gratifying and obliging them with such unreasonable things as otherwise [the senators] would have felt it honourable for them to incur the greatest unpopularity in resisting]. Livius offering to pleasure the Senate with his authority, preferred laws neither honourable nor profitable to the commonwealth, and [that] were to no other end, but contending with Gaius, who should most flatter the people of them two, as players do in their common plays, to shew the people pastime.

Whereby the Senate shewed, that they did not so much mislike Gaius' doings, as for the desire they had to overthrow him and his great credit with the people. For where Gaius preferred but the replenishing of the two cities, and desired to send the honestest citizens thither: they objected against him, that he did corrupt the common people. On the other side, also they favoured Drusus, who preferred a law that they should replenish twelve colonies, and should send to every one of them three thousand of the poorest citizens. And where they hated Gaius for that he had charged the poor citizens with an annual rent for the lands that were divided unto them: Livius in contrary manner did please them by disburdening them of that rent and payment, letting them have the lands scot free.

Narration and Discussion

In **Part One**, Gaius supported his friend Gaius Fannius in the election for consul. By **Part Two**, Fannius is called a "slack friend." What might have happened during that time?

Explain the game of one-upmanship that the senators began against Gaius. Did they actually dislike the things he was proposing?

For older students: North's choice of phrase "**as if he had had but one master in hand**" has interesting connotations; but Dryden translates it "as if he had been but engaged upon one [undertaking]." Both translations echo what Charlotte Mason described in her book *Ourselves*: "The simple, rectified Will, what our Lord calls 'the single eye,' would appear to be the one thing needful for straight living and serviceableness." What are the benefits, and possibly the dangers, of such single-mindedness?

Lesson Ten

Introduction

In this lesson, we are introduced to Marcus Fulvius Flaccus. Fulvius was involved in the administration of the *Lex Agraria*; had been a consul for a year and earned a military triumph; and finally took the unusual step of becoming a tribune so that he could support the proposals of Gaius Gracchus. But his loyalty to Gaius became a threat to his own safety, and vice versa.

Vocabulary

scourge: whip

a seditious man: Dryden, "a man of a turbulent spirit"

incontinently: immediately

to speed: to have a good chance of being chosen

set Gaius beside the saddle: get him out of the way

he removed from his house: he moved his residence

repairing to Rome out of all parts...: coming to the city to vote

People

Fannius: see **Lesson Nine**

Lucius Opimius: consul in 121 B.C. along with Fabius

Reading

Part One

Furthermore also, where Gaius did anger the people, because he gave all the Latins the freedom of Rome to give their voices in choosing of magistrates as freely as the natural Romans: when Drusus on the other side had preferred a law that thenceforth no Roman should [**scourge** a Latin soldier], they liked the law, and passed it. Livius also, in every law he put forth, said in all his orations that he did it by the counsel of the Senate, who were very careful for the profit of the people: and this was all the good he did in his office unto the commonwealth. For by his means the people were better pleased with the Senate, and where they did before hate all the noblemen of the Senate, Livius took away that malice, when the people saw that all that he propounded was for the preferment and benefit of the commonwealth, with the consent and furtherance of the Senate.

The only thing also that persuaded the people to think that Drusus meant uprightly, and that he only respected the profit of the common people, was that he never preferred any law for himself, or for his own benefit. For in the restoring of these colonies which he preferred, he always sent other commissioners, and gave them the charge of it, and would never finger any money himself: where Gaius took upon him the charge and care of all things himself, and specially of the greatest matters.

Rubrius also, another tribune, having preferred a law for the re-edifying and replenishing of Carthage again with people, the which Scipio [*the Younger*] had razed and destroyed: it was Gaius' hap to be appointed one of the commissioners for it. Whereupon he took ship, and sailed into Africa. Drusus in the meantime taking occasion of his absence, did as much as might be to seek the favour of the common people, and specially by accusing **Fulvius**, who was one of the best friends Gaius had, and whom they had also chosen commissioner with him for the division of these lands among the citizens, whom they sent to replenish these colonies. This Fulvius was **a seditious man**, and therefore marvellously hated of the Senate, and withal suspected also [by] them that took part with the people, that he secretly practised to make their confederates of Italy to rebel. But yet they had no evident proofs of it to justify it against him, more than that which he himself did verify, [than his being an unsettled character and of a well-known seditious temper]. And this was one of the chiefest causes of Gaius' overthrow, [for part of the envy which fell upon Fulvius was extended to him].

[A flashback to 129 B.C.]

For when Scipio Africanus [*the Younger*] was found dead one morning in his house, without any manifest cause how he should come to his death so suddenly: (saving that there appeared certain blind marks of stripes on his body that had been given him: as we have declared at large in his *Life*) the most part of the suspicion of his death was laid to Fulvius, being his mortal enemy, and because the same day they had been at great words together in the pulpit for orations. So was Gaius Gracchus also partly suspected for it. Howsoever it was, such a horrible murder as this, of so famous and worthy a man as any was in Rome, was yet notwithstanding never revenged, neither any inquiry made of it: because the common people would not suffer the accusation to go forward, fearing lest Gaius would be found in fault, if the matter should go forward. But this was a great while before.

Part Two

Now Gaius at that time being in Africa about the re-edifying and replenishing of the city of Carthage again, the which he named *Colonia Iunonia*: the voice goeth that he had many ill signs and tokens appeared unto him. For the staff of his ensign was broken with a vehement blast of wind, and with the force of the ensign bearer that held it fast on the other side. There came a [sudden storm] also that carried away the sacrifices upon the altars and blew them quite out of the circuit which was marked out for the compass of the city. Furthermore, the wolves came [and carried away the very marks that were set up to show the boundary].

This notwithstanding, Gaius having dispatched all things in the space of three score and ten days, he returned **incontinently** to Rome, understanding that Fulvius was [prosecuted] by Drusus, and that those matters required his presence. For **Lucius Opimius** that was all in all for the nobility, and a man of great credit with the Senate, being the year before put by the consulship, by Gaius' practise, who caused Fannius to be chosen: he had good hope this year **to speed**, for the great number of friends that furthered his suit. So that if he could obtain it, he was fully bent to **set Gaius beside the saddle**, and the rather, because his [Gaius's] estimation and countenance he was wont to have among the people, began now to decay, [because there were so many others who every day contrived new ways to please them, with which the Senate readily complied].

So Gaius being returned to Rome, **he removed from his house**, and where before he dwelt in Mount Palatine, he came now to take a house under the marketplace, to shew himself thereby the lowlier and more popular, because many of the meaner sort of people dwelt thereabouts. Then he purposed to go forward with the rest of his laws, and to make the people to establish them, a great number of people **repairing to Rome out of all parts for the furtherance thereof**. Howbeit the Senate counselled the consul Fannius to make proclamation, that all those which were no natural Romans, resident and abiding within the city [it]self of Rome: that they should depart out of Rome. Besides all this, there was a strange proclamation made, and never seen before: that none of all the friends and confederates of the Romans, [during that time], should come into Rome. But Gaius on the the other side set up bills on every post, accusing the consul for making so wicked a proclamation: and further, promised the confederates of Rome to aid them, if they would remain there against the consul's proclamation. But yet he performed it not. For when he saw one of Fannius' sergeants carry a friend of his to prison, he held on his way, and would see nothing, neither did he help him: either of likelihood because he feared his credit with the people, which began to decay, or else because he was [unwilling] (as he said) to pick any quarrel with his enemies, which sought it of him.

Narration and Discussion

Drusus preferred to keep his hands away from the public money. Was he honest, lazy, or afraid to risk criticism?

How did Gaius' friendship with Fulvius affect his own standing in Rome? What other reasons are given for the decline in his popularity?

Lesson Eleven

Introduction

Now that Gaius was no longer tribune, the Senate felt free to revoke his laws, partly to provoke him into violent or illegal action. Gaius held out patiently for as long as he could, but the tension in Rome was mounting. When a rude remark blew into a fight and then murder, the frightened Senate put the city under full control of the new consul Opimius.

Vocabulary

sword players or fencers at the sharp: gladiators

scaffolds: grandstands; raised seating (which also obscured the view of the bystanders)

bold presumptuous man: particularly because he had dishonoured another tribune by his actions

he was put from his third tribuneship: Gaius and Fulvius had lost their positions as tribunes, Opimius had been elected consul for 121 B.C., and Fannius was not re-elected consul.

voices: votes

bodkins to write with: Death by writing implement sounds strange, but Roman styluses could be sharp.

extraordinary power and authority: *Senatus consultum ultimum*, or "Final Act"; a lifting of limits on magisterial power that had never been used before

betimes: early

at such a strait: at such a dangerous time

to take Mount Aventine: to make this spot the centre of a protest against the "Final Act"

lay flatling: lay prostrate on the ground

Reading

Part One

Furthermore, he chanced to fall at variance with his brethren the tribunes, about this occasion. The people were to see the pastime of the **sword players or fencers at the sharp**, within the very marketplace, and there were divers of the officers that to see the sport, did set up **scaffolds** round about, to take money for the standing. Gaius commanded them to take them down again, because the poor men might see the sport without any cost. But not a man of them would yield to it. Wherefore he stayed till the night before the pastime should be, and then he took all his labourers he had under him, and went and overthrew the scaffolds every one of them: so that the next morning all the marketplace was clear for the common people, to see the pastime at their pleasure. For this fact of his, the people thanked him marvellously, and took him for a worthy man. Howbeit his brethren the tribunes were very much offended with him, and took him for a **bold presumptuous man**.

This seemeth to be the chief cause why **he was put from his third tribuneship**, where he had the most **voices** of his side: because his colleagues, to be revenged of the part he had played them, of malice and spite made false report of the **voices**. Howbeit there is no great truth in this. Furthermore, his enemies having chosen Opimius [as] consul, they began immediately to revoke divers of Gaius' laws: as among the rest, his doings at Carthage for the re-edifying of that city, procuring thus all the ways they could to anger him, because they might have just occasion of anger to kill him. Gaius notwithstanding did patiently bear it at the first: but afterwards his friends, and specially Fulvius, did encourage him so, that he began again to gather men to resist the consul.

When the day came that they should proceed to the revocation of his laws, both parties met by break of day at the Capitol. There when the consul Opimius had done sacrifice, [an attendant on the consul], called Quintus Antyllius, carrying the entrails of the beast sacrificed, said unto Fulvius, and others of his tribe that were about him: "Give place to honest men, vile citizens that ye be." Some say also, that besides these injurious words, in scorn and contempt, he held out his naked arm [in scorn and contempt]. Whereupon they slew him

[Antyllius] presently in the field with great **bodkins to write with**, which they had purposely made for that intent.

Hereupon the common people were marvellously offended for this murder, and the chief men of both sides also were diversely affected. For Gaius was very sorry for it, and bitterly reproved them that were about him, saying, that they had given their enemies the occasion they looked for, to set upon them. [Opimius, immediately seizing the occasion thus offered, was in great delight, and urged the people to revenge.] But there fell a shower of rain at that time that parted them.

Part Two

The next morning, the consul having assembled the Senate by break of day, as he was dispatching causes within, some had taken the body of Antyllius and laid it naked upon the bier, and so carried it through the marketplace (as it was agreed upon before amongst them) and brought it to the Senate door: where they began to make great moan and lamentation, Opimius knowing the meaning of it, but yet he [seemed to be surprised, and wondered what the meaning of it should be].

Whereupon the senators went out to see what it was, and finding this bier, in the marketplace, some fell a-weeping for him that was dead, others cried out that it was a shameful act, and in no wise to be suffered. But on the other side, this did revive the old grudge and malice of the people, for the wickedness of the ambitious noblemen: who having themselves before slain Tiberius Gracchus that was tribune, and within the Capitol itself, and had also cast his body into the river, did now make an honourable show openly in the marketplace, of the body of [an ordinary hired attendant] (who though he were wrongfully slain, yet had himself given them the cause that slew him, to do that [which] they did); and all the whole Senate were about the bier to bewail his death, and to honour the funerals of a hireling, to make the people also kill him [Gaius], that was only left the protector and defender of the people.

After this, they [*the senators*] went again unto the Capitol, and there made a decree, whereby they gave the consul Opimius **extraordinary power and authority**, by absolute power to provide for the safety of the commonwealth, to preserve the city, and to suppress the tyrants.

This decree being established, the consul presently commanded the senators that were present there to go arm themselves: and appointed the Roman knights, that the next morning **betimes** every man should bring two of their men armed with them. Fulvius, on the other side, prepared his force against them, and assembled the common people together. Gaius also returning from the marketplace, stayed before the image of his father, and looked earnestly upon it without ever a word speaking, only he burst out a-weeping, and fetching a great sigh, went his way. This made the people to pity him that saw him: so that they talked among themselves, that they were but beasts and cowards **at such a strait** to forsake so worthy a man. Thereupon they went to his house, stayed there all night and watched before his gate: not as they did that watched with Fulvius, that passed away the night in guzzling and drinking drunk, crying out, and making noise, Fulvius himself being drunk first of all, who both spake and did many thinges fain unmeet for his calling. For they that watched Gaius, on the other side, were very sorrowful, and made no noise, even as in a common calamity of their country, devising with themselves what would fall out upon it, waking, and sleeping one after another by turns.

When the day broke, they with Fulvius did awake him, who slept yet soundly for the wine he drank overnight. They armed themselves with the spoils of the Gauls that hung round about his house, whom he had overcome in battle the same year he was consul: and with great cries, and thundering threats, they went **to take Mount Aventine**. But Gaius would not arm himself, but went out of his house in a long gown, as if he would have gone simply into the marketplace according to his wonted manner, saving that he carried a short dagger at his girdle under his gown. So as he was going out of his house, his wife stayed him at the door, and holding him by the one hand, and a little child of his in her other hand, she said thus unto him:

"Alas Gaius, thou dost not now go as thou wert
wont, [as] a tribune into the marketplace to speak to
the people, neither to prefer any new laws: neither
dost thou go unto an honest war, that if
unfortunately that should happen to thee that is
common to all men, I might yet at the least mourn
for thy death with honour. But thou goest to put

thyself into bloody butchers' hands, who most cruelly have slain thy brother Tiberius: and yet thou goest, a naked man unarmed, intending rather to suffer, than to do hurt. Besides, thy death can bring no benefit to the commonwealth. For the worser part hath now the upper hand, considering that sentence passeth by force of sword. Had thy brother been slain by his enemies, before the city of Numantia: yet had they given us his body to have buried him. But such may be my misfortune, that I may presently go to pray the river or sea to give me thy body, which as thy brother's they have likewise thrown into the same. Alas, what hope or trust is left us now, in laws or gods, since they have slain Tiberius?"

As Licinia was making this pitiful moan unto him, Gaius fair and softly pulled his hand from her, and left her, giving her never a word, but went on with his friends. But she reaching after him to take him by the gown, fell to the ground, and **lay flatling** there a great while, speaking never a word: until at length her servants took her up in a swoon, and carried her so unto her brother Crassus.

Narration and Discussion

Why did the senators take such extreme measures at this time? What were their worst fears?

Creative narration: Compare the ways that Fulvius and Tiberius spent the night before the final events of this story. You might write a monologue for each of them.

Lesson Twelve

Introduction:

Outlawed by Roman authorities, Gaius and his supporters now had no choice but to fight fiercely for their lives.

Vocabulary

hothouse: possibly a workshop or a bathing house

turned their coats: deserted, shifted their loyalty

jointure: dowry

Historic Occasions

121 B.C.: the death of Gaius Gracchus

Reading

Part One

Now Fulvius, by the persuasion of Gaius, when all their faction were met, sent his younger son (which was a pretty fair boy) [into the marketplace], with a herald's rod in his hand for his safety. This boy humbly presenting his duty, with the tears in his eyes, before the consul and Senate, offered them peace. The most of them that were present thought very well of it. But Opimius made answer, saying that it became them not to send messengers, thinking with fair words to win the Senate: but it was their duty to come themselves in persons, like subjects and offenders to make their trial, and so to crave pardon, and to seek to pacify the wrath of the Senate. Then he commanded the boy he should not return again to them, but with this condition he had prescribed. Gaius (as it is reported) was ready to go and clear himself unto the Senate: but [none of his friends consented to it].

Whereupon Fulvius sent his son back again unto them, to speak for them as he had done before. But Opimius, that was desirous to fight, caused the boy to be taken, and committed him in safe custody; and then went presently against Fulvius with a great number of footmen well armed, and of Cretan archers besides: who with their arrows did more trouble and hurt their enemies, than with anything else, [so that a rout and flight quickly ensued]. Fulvius, on the other side, fled into an old **hothouse** that nobody made reckoning of, and there being found shortly after, they slew him, and his eldest son.

185

Now for Gaius, he fought not at all, but being mad with himself, and grieved to see such bloodshed: he got him into the temple of Diana, where he would have killed himself, had not his very good friends Pomponius and Licinius saved him. For both they being with him at that time, took his sword from him, and counselled him to flee. It is reported that then he fell down on his knees, and holding up both his hands unto the goddess, he besought her that the people might never come out of bondage, to be revenged of this their ingratitude and treason. For the common people (or the most part of them) plainly **turned their coats**, when they heard proclamation made that all men had pardon granted them, that would return.

[Gaius, therefore, endeavoured now to make his escape], and his enemies followed him so near, that they overtook him upon the wooden bridge, where two of his friends that were with him stayed, to defend him against his followers, and bade him in the meantime make shift for himself, whilst they fought with them upon the bridge: and so they did, and kept them that not a man got the bridge of them, until they were both slain. Now there was none that fled with Gaius, but one of his men called Philocrates: notwithstanding, every man did still encourage and counsel him, as they do men to win a game, but no man would help him, nor offer him any horse, though he often required it, because he saw his enemies so near unto him.

This notwithstanding, by their defence that were slain upon the bridge, he got ground on them so that he had leisure to creep into a little grove of wood which was consecrated to the Furies. There his servant Philocrates slew him, and then slew himself also, and fell dead upon him. Other[s] write, notwithstanding, that both the master and servant were overtaken, and taken alive: and that his servant did so straight embrace his master that none of the enemies could strike him for all the blows they gave, before he was slain himself.

The bodies of these two men, Gaius Gracchus and Fulvius, and of [their other] followers (which were to the number of three thousand that were slain) were all thrown into the river, their goods confiscate[d], and their widows forbidden to mourn for their death. Furthermore, they took from Licinia, Gaius' wife, her **jointure**: but yet they dealt more cruelly and beastly with the young boy, Fulvius' son: who had neither lift[ed] up his hand against them, nor was in the fight among them, but only came to them to make peace before they fought, whom they kept as prisoner, and after the battle ended, they put him to death.

But yet that which most of all other grieved the people, was the Temple of Concord, the which Opimius caused to be built: for it appeared that he boasted, and in manner triumphed, that he had slain so many citizens of Rome. And therefore there were [some] that in the night wrote under the inscription of the temple these verses:

A furious fact and full of beastly shame.

This temple built, that beareth Concord's name.

Part Two

This Opimius was the first man at Rome, that being consul, usurped the absolute power of the dictator: and that without law or justice condemned three thousand citizens of Rome, besides Fulvius Flaccus (who had also been consul, and had received the honour of triumph), and Gaius Gracchus, a young man in like case, who in virtue and reputation excelled all the men of his years. [Afterwards he was found incapable of keeping his hands from thieving.] For when he was sent [as] ambassador unto Jugurtha, king of Numidia, he was bribed with money; and thereupon being accused, he was most shamefully convicted, and condemned. Wherefore he ended his days with this reproach and infamy, hated, and mocked of all the people; because at the time of the overthrow he dealt beastly with them that fought for his quarrel.

But shortly after, it appeared to the world how much they lamented the loss of the two brethren of the Gracchi. For they made images and statues of them, and caused them to be set up in an open and honourable place, consecrating the places where they had been slain: and many of them also came and offered to them, of their first fruits and flowers, according to the time of the year, and went thither to make their prayers on their knees, as unto the temples of the gods. Their mother Cornelia, as writers report, did bear this calamity with a noble heart: and as for the chapels which they built and consecrated unto them in the place where they were slain, she said no more, but that they had such graves as they had deserved.

Afterwards she dwelt continually by the Mount of Misene, and never changed her manner of life. She had many friends, and because she was a noble lady, and loved ever to welcome strangers, she kept a very good house, and therefore had always great repair unto her of Grecians and learned men: besides, there was no king nor prince, but both received gifts from her, and sent [*gifts to*] her again. They that frequented her company, delighted marvellously to hear her report the deeds and manner of her father's life, Scipio Africanus [*the Elder*]: but yet they wondered more, to hear her tell the acts and death of her two sons, Tiberius and Gaius Gracchi, without shedding [a] tear, or making any shew of lamentation or grief, no more than if she had told an history unto them that had requested her. Insomuch some writers report, that age, or her great misfortunes, had overcome and taken her reason and sense from her, to feel any sorrow. But indeed they were senseless to say so, not understanding, how that to be nobly born, and virtuously brought up, doth make men temperately to digest sorrow, and that fortune oftentimes overcomes virtue, which regardeth honesty in all respects, but yet with any adversity she [fortune] cannot take away the temperance from them, whereby they patiently bear it.

[*Dryden translates the last lines this way: "and though fortune may often be more successful, and may defeat the efforts of virtue to avert misfortunes, it cannot, when we incur them, prevent our bearing them reasonably."*]

Narration and Discussion

Why did Gaius' friends encourage but not help him?

North refers in the last sentence to "temperance." What sort of temperance did Plutarch mean? Why was it hard for others to understand Cornelia's acceptance of tragedy?

The Impact of the Gracchi

After this uprising, and the subsequent purge of three thousand people, Roman reaction turned to regret. Two Gracchi brothers put to death by angry mobs seemed like two too many; not to mention the many other lives lost. What impact did they have on the laws of Rome, or on the rights of citizens to have a voice? Were their efforts worth the cost of their lives?

Bibliography

Plutarch's Lives of the Noble Greeks and Romans. Englished by Sir Thomas North. With an introduction by George Wyndham. Fifth Volume. London: Dent, 1894. (Julius Caesar, Agis and Cleomenes, Tiberius and Caius Gracchi) https://archive.org/details/livesofnoblegrec05plut

Plutarch's Lives: The Dryden Plutarch. Revised by Arthur Hugh Clough. Volume 2. London: J.M. Dent, 1910. (Caesar) https://archive.org/details/plutarchslives02plut

Plutarch's Lives: The Dryden Plutarch. Revised by Arthur Hugh Clough. Volume 3. London: J.M. Dent, 1910. (Agis, Cleomenes, Tiberius Gracchus, Caius Gracchus) https://archive.org/details/plutarchslives03plut

About the Author

Anne E. White (www.annewrites.ca) has shared her knowledge of Charlotte Mason's methods through magazine columns, online writing, and conference workshops. She is an Advisory member of AmblesideOnline, and the author of *Minds More Awake: The Vision of Charlotte Mason*, as well as other books in The Plutarch Project series.

Made in the USA
Lexington, KY
29 July 2017